BUZZ

BUZZ
How to Create It and Win with It

Edward I. Koch
and Christy Heady

AMACOM

American Management Association
New York • Atlanta • Brussels • Chicago • Mexico City • San Francisco
Shanghai • Tokyo • Toronto • Washington, D.C.

Special discounts on bulk quantities of AMACOM books are available to corporations, professional associations, and other organizations. For details, contact Special Sales Department, AMACOM, a division of American Management Association, 1601 Broadway, New York, NY 10019.
Tel: 212-903-8316. Fax: 212-903-8083.
E-mail: specialsls@amanet.org
Website: www.amacombooks.org/go/specialsales
To view all AMACOM titles go to: www.amacombooks.org

This publication is designed to provide accurate and authoritative information in regard to the subject matter covered. It is sold with the understanding that the publisher is not engaged in rendering legal, accounting, or other professional service. If legal advice or other expert assistance is required, the services of a competent professional person should be sought.

Library of Congress Cataloging-in-Publication Data

Koch, Ed, 1924–
    Buzz : how to create it and win with it / Edward I. Koch and Christy Heady.
        p.   cm.
    Includes index.
    ISBN-13: 978-0-8144-7462-4
    ISBN-10: 0-8144-7462-4
    1. Success in business.   2. Success.   3. Interpersonal communication.   4. Persuasion (Psychology)   I. Heady, Christy. II. Title.

    HF5386.K758   2007
    658.4'09—dc22   2007009714

Printing number

10   9   8   7   6   5   4   3   2   1

Dedication

I love the City of New York. It is not the most beautiful, Paris is. It is not the most interesting, London is. But it is the most electrifying, and because of our immigration laws, its population makes it the most diverse city in the world.

When I had a stroke in 1987, I had a conversation with God. I said, I'm not afraid to go when I am called, but please take me all at once—no salami tactics—and I will devote the rest of my life to public service. He has kept His part of the agreement to date, and I have kept mine, serving both in and out of government. The people of New York City have provided me with extraordinary opportunities, for which I shall be forever grateful. This book is dedicated to them.

Contents

Acknowledgments

I am very grateful to Christy Heady, who has made writing this book a dream.

I am also very fortunate to have two crackerjack assistants: Mary Garrigan, who began working with me in 1975 when I was a congressman, and Jody Smith, who joined my office in 1995. I couldn't get anything done without them.

BUZZ

INTRODUCTION

In 1963, I was a relative newcomer to politics and ran for Democratic District Leader in Greenwich Village against Carmine DeSapio. DeSapio had been the powerful Democratic County Leader of Manhattan, but was defeated two years earlier by James Lannigan. Now I was running against DeSapio, who was seeking to run again for district leader.

Taking on DeSapio was no easy task. He had lived in Greenwich Village for most of his life, was known everywhere, and had the local ethnic Italian support and enormous financial resources. I was not well known and was a relative newcomer to the Village. DeSapio enhanced his political chances by circulating prominently in social groups and supporting public issues proposed by the middle-class Jewish community, who had given him their support in the past. My duty was to make myself known to the Greenwich Village Democrats, who would be voting in the primary that year.

To do so I had to create some "buzz" and become known. I literally would stand on a box in Sheridan Square and talk to fifty to seventy-five people who were willing to stop and listen to me for about a half-hour—something I learned how to do when campaigning for Adlai Stevenson for president in 1952 and 1956.

Many of the people listening to me were residents of the Village, and many of them were Italian-Americans expected again to vote for DeSapio on an ethnic basis.

Here I was, a Jewish lawyer born in the Bronx who had in 1956 moved from my parental home in Brooklyn, taking on an Italian among Italian-American voters. I would say, particularly when speaking to the mostly Italian South Villagers, "Carmine deserted you when he moved from the South Village [below Washington Square Park] to 11 Fifth Avenue [just north of Washington Square Park]." I attacked DeSapio for moving seven or so blocks from one address in the Village to another, and attacked him unmercifully for moving "uptown."

Believe it or not, the Italian-Americans liked what I said, respected me for it, and funny as it may seem today—my charge against DeSapio of deserting his "neighborhood" was reason enough for some living in the South Village to not vote for him for district leader. I won by a majority of 41 votes out of the 9,000 or so cast.

I was now District Leader Ed Koch. My success happened, I believe, because I caught the public's attention. And, of course, I was supported by hundreds of dedicated Greenwich Village reformers at the Village Independent Democrats (VID) club.

The skills I honed during that campaign I have used for decades.

Even today, to make a point I tell anecdotes about everyday incidents. These require timing, something I do very well and have in abundance. The stories I tell are true, short, direct, never contrived, and funny. That's not to say I don't enjoy listening to a good joke, but I am not comfortable retelling them, and so I never, and I mean never, repeat a joke.

When I ran for mayor, I told a story to a group of 200 senior citizens. "Ladies and gentlemen," I began, "there is only one issue in this campaign, and you and I know that issue is crime. A judge I know was recently mugged, and do you know what he did? He called a press conference and said to the reporters, 'This mugging of me will in no way affect my decisions in matters of this kind.'"

An elderly woman in the group, with a heavy Central European Jewish accent, rose from her seat and exclaimed, "Then mug him again."

The entire audience cheered, whistled, and stomped their feet. I had them in my corner and they were mine forever. I told that story a thousand times during that campaign, which resulted in huge numbers of seniors supporting me.

I don't believe the word "buzz" was used in the days when I decided to run for public and party office. Today, I not only use the word, but I think it's fair to say that I can create one when I enter a room. There is an expectation that I will stop and talk, and that I will say something on target that will cause the people in the room to identify with me and me with them.

Perhaps a non sequitur, and perhaps not: When recently I entered a room, a middle-aged woman said to me, "They told me that you were smart, but they didn't tell me that you were gorgeous." I can't top that.

In politics, creating a buzz is about making a memorable entrance by not letting the crowd forget who you are and what you stand for.

My most vivid memory of a public figure that best represents this was the former first lady, Jackie Kennedy Onassis. During the early 1970s, when I was a member of Congress and living and working in Washington, D.C., I was invited to a performance at the Kennedy Center. I watched with amazement how Jackie, surrounded by fifty or more photographers, walked from one side of the room to the other, having her photograph taken the whole time. This mystique she held for the public and, therefore, for the media, was unique. She was the center of the room.

To watch a political figure create buzz is mesmerizing. Political figures often try to create interest in themselves for obvious reasons. They want, indeed need, people to know them and their names. But fair warning—much danger exists when embarking on a career, especially a political one, without knowing the ins and outs of good strategic "buzz" planning. Why? Depending on your approach, you may come across as too aggressive, too pushy, or perhaps disrespectful of others' rights. Even worse is to become a ludicrous figure, mocked, or perceived as a fool. There are a number of people in public office now or in the past who are famous for popping up and getting in the picture celebrating a political event they had little or nothing to do with. Those who become known for doing that pay an awful price—ridicule.

Today, the word "buzz" is used to describe the commotion created by a number of well-known people when they enter a public venue. Generally speaking, creating buzz is no more than stirring the pot in order to stand out.

Some folks may call it "good, strategic PR." Others may say that buzz is defined as common sense with heavy doses of energetic passion and keen observation.

No matter what the definition, you want to become known, if possible, by both face and name.

Whether you're running for public office, wishing to advance to the top of your firm, providing first-class service to your customers, or leading a group of people to help generate community activism—honesty, integrity, and ethics are essential to my version of buzz.

These principles are some of the ingredients that have allowed me to maintain a very successful and long-time career in politics and the law. And I still use them today. For example, I am a proud and lifelong Democrat, yet I made no secret of my choice for president of the United States during the November 2004 presidential election. My reasons were honest, open, and clear, and I was quite vocal about it. In January of 2004, I wrote in the *Forward*, a newspaper with a large Jewish readership, how the threat of international terrorism far outweighed my disagreement with President George W. Bush on all of the domestic issues. Indeed, I said I did not agree with the president on a single domestic issue, ranging from tax policy to prescription drugs.

I was asked to speak at the Republican National Convention, to both introduce Mayor Michael Bloomberg and endorse President Bush. I accepted the invitation and was cheered when I appeared. My endorsement of the president was both substantive and funny. I said:

> *I'm Ed Koch. (APPLAUSE) I know what you're thinking. What's Ed Koch doing at the Republican convention? Me, a Democratic district leader in Greenwich Village, Democratic city council member, a Democratic member of Congress, a Democratic mayor.*
>
> *Why am I here? I'm here to convert you. (LAUGHTER) But that's for the next election. This year, I'm voting for the reelection of President George W. Bush. How'm I doing? (APPLAUSE) When I was asked to lead the campaign to recruit 8,000 volunteers to make the convention a success, I said, "Of course." I did a TV commercial. Perhaps you saw it. It starred Minnie, the Republican elephant, and me. (LAUGHTER)*
>
> *Let me tell you a secret: Making that commercial violated a commitment I made almost sixty years ago, not to the Democrats, but to my sainted mother who told me, "Eddie, never fool around with a wild animal." But I did it for New York. (APPLAUSE) I did it because I want every single delegate and guest to go back home and tell everyone, I had the time of my life and I really love New York. (APPLAUSE) Hey, you don't have to believe me. See for yourself.*

My choice for President of the United States generated great media attention. Ads for the Republican National Convention showcased me and Minnie the elephant with the slogan, "You don't have to be a Democrat to love New York."

I have witnessed dozens of successful business people, politicians, and the media work together to make a proactive fuss, be it about a cause, a person, or an event. I have also found when buzz principles aren't used in tandem, buzz still happens, but it may not be to your liking.

That's why I am writing this book. With *Buzz: How to Create It and Win with It*, I want to teach you how to become a successful buzz magnet and self-marketing machine to achieve your goals and win!

Using my experiences, I'll share strategies with you on how to create a successful word-of-mouth crusade. You will also learn how to successfully ride out those rough times and spot the lessons to learn when the buzz isn't so good. My goal is that you find this book stimulating and educational.

This book is divided into four parts. Here's how it works:

Part One: *How Buzz Begins* grounds you in the basics. It informs and helps you discern the necessary, can't-do-without principles required in making a difference in your career.

Part Two: *Creating a Stir* teaches you how to create a step-by-step personal and professional development plan that will attract the media and identify your cheerleaders.

Part Three: *Trusting Your Plan* provides you with the insight to really rely on yourself to take that next leap of faith to stick to your plan and enforce your philosophies. This section also gives you inside strategies to transform mistakes into wise decision-making for the future.

Part Four: *Recognizing Victory* gives you key insights into how to handle triumphs and public pitfalls, and be open to change.

Within these chapters, you will find useful side notes that will give you brief tips and advice. You'll also learn which dangerous and costly traps to avoid.

Whatever your professional path in life, I want to help you carve out your area of expertise so that when people discuss a particular discipline, they include you among those they should look to for guidance.

Some people undoubtedly have not liked what I have to say, but I have always strived to leave a positive mark for future generations and to never frame my remarks without including the sting of candor. Even those hostile to me know I am both intellectually and financially honest.

If you read nothing more than the introduction to this book, remember this: Apply yourself, learn as much as possible, and be sure you have all the facts when discussing a topic. And never exaggerate your knowledge. This last principle is based on my rule of thumb—an assumption that served me well as mayor: 70 percent of what people tell you is pure B.S. If the person is an expert, perhaps it's only 30 percent. (Today, on reflection, I think it is considerably less.) If you want to get the truth, get it in writing and then there is a great chance that only 10 percent will be B.S.—the irreducible minimum.

I hope you enjoy this book. All the best.

Edward I. Koch

Part One

HOW BUZZ BEGINS

The buzz I create comes as a result of being provocative, thoughtful, and factual.

If someone were to ask me where my passion for creating buzz comes from, I'd say it's self-taught and self-induced. People trust me. I have a special relationship with New York City and its people, and I love it. I have not—and will not ever—betray those who have put their trust in me.

I have been fortunate, too. Most people at 82 are retired. Few continue to be gainfully employed. I often make the comment and I am proud to say, "I still pay Social Security taxes on my earned income." My income continues to put me in the category of the top 1 to 2 percent of taxpayers in this country, so my buzz obviously still works.

And yours can, too. Some of you may be working with public relations firms or marketing executives to help carry out your message. Remember, though, you are your own expert. You are the one on whom you will ultimately rely to carry out your mission of creating and nurturing the best buzz possible. I hope this book will help you.

Chapter One

HONESTY COMES FIRST

I am always amazed at how many people want my opinion, because I can be brutally honest. No doubt about it—I am blunt. I do try to forewarn them about this character trait of mine by asking, "Do you really want to know?" They always say yes, and then often don't like my response. They really didn't want to know.

Being honest is key to my lifelong goal, which is to remain relevant. I like to think intellectual and financial honesty are in my DNA. Candor—an honest response to a question—is one of my character strengths. I believe that because of my honesty and candor I have succeeded.

I am shocked that more than seventeen years after leaving public office, the public still recalls me fondly and, apparently, is still interested in my views. An independent verification of this comes from a poll taken in September 2005 by radio station 1010 WINS of the Top 40 Newsmakers in New York City. I am listed as number 3. Rudy Giuliani was number 1. Current Mayor Mike Bloomberg—before his reelection—was number 15. Hillary Clinton's number was 20. Frank Sinatra was num-

I lost when I ran for a fourth term as mayor. At the end of 1989, the people threw me out, electing David Dinkins. However, candidates for political office in New York City and State—mostly Democrats, but a few Republicans as well—continue to seek my endorsement in large numbers.

Several of the candidates I endorsed in 2005 and 2006 were (in alphabetical order):

- Michael Bloomberg (Republican) for New York City mayor (reelection)
- Hillary Clinton for the U.S. Senate (reelection)
- Andrew Cuomo for New York State Attorney General
- Daniel Garodnick for City Council District 4
- Rory Lancman for New York State Assembly
- Eve Rachel Markewich for Manhattan Surrogate Court Judge
- Eliot Spitzer for New York State Governor
- Scott Stringer for Manhattan Borough President

ber 10. Jerry Seinfeld was number 24, and Donald Trump (the only fly in the ointment) was number 4.

While I have never referred to myself as a brand, my imprimatur does have an impact to the point where I have been retained under contract to do a number of television commercials. I have done commercials and endorsements for products such as Slim-Fast, HIP health insurance, Citibank check card, Dunkin Donuts, General Tire, Snapple, and FreshDirect.

In fact, FreshDirect, the online grocery service that delivers freshly cooked meals and groceries throughout most of New York City, New Jersey, and Westchester County, called my agent at William Morris. They wanted me to do a TV commercial. They also were courting celebrity chef Bobby Flay and supermodel Paulina Porizkova. The commercials ran on a number of stations and were a big hit.

I loved my speaking line created by the writers. I say of FreshDirect, "It's the best thing to ever happen to New York. Okay, maybe the second." I thought it was first-rate. It seemed to be perceived that way by everyone at FreshDirect as well.

A number of months later, the company wanted to use my picture on telephone booths around the city. We could not agree on a price to be paid to me, so as of this writing, FreshDirect has engaged two other persons for their commercials—Spike Lee and Cynthia Nixon. Their commercials, which began in late 2006, are very good, but I honestly think mine is far better in conveying good humor and honesty.

My candor and my common sense views have allowed me to become and enjoy being popular. People may not always agree with me, but they will always know where I stand—without question. My self-introduction on my call-in radio show includes the phrase, "Ed Koch, the voice of reason." I am a moderate in my views. My views on controversial matters have become more educated but have not changed dramatically with the passage of time. That may be a flaw—not to substantially change one's points of view with age—but I honestly don't think so.

Why am I such a buzz magnet? I'd like to reiterate that it's due to the two traits that are not the coin of the realm—intellectual and financial honesty. I'm not a scientist, but for me I even think those traits are genetic. I cannot understand why people would not choose to follow the path of integrity.

The Perceived Honesty of Public Officials

In April 2006, a USA Today/Gallup poll reported that 44 percent of adults nationwide think corruption in Congress is a somewhat serious problem. The public generally believes most if not all public officials are intellectually and financially dishonest, but they also believe that their own elected official is honest. In my opinion, most public officials are honest financially; they are constantly under observation and comment by government monitors and opponents.

Are we living in a culture of corruption? I believe that political corruption does indeed play a significant role in the decision-making process of any voter. I have repeatedly stated to audiences —before, during, and after elections—that "public service is the noblest of professions, if done honestly and done well." Americans believe that large numbers of politicians are corrupt. The truth is, I believe, that as a group, politicians are less corrupt than the population from which they come.

The reason is that they are constantly being looked at and questioned. That happens in campaigns when their adversaries and the media are constantly scrutinizing what they've done and said. There are law enforcement agencies looking at and very willing to pursue public officeholders when allegations or charges are aired publicly or filed with the agencies. These agencies include district attorneys, U.S. Attorneys, and—unique to New York City—the Department of Investigation, a city agency created long ago to actively look for corruption in the ranks of city employees.

Nevertheless, while most city employees are honest, a conversation that I had when I was mayor with the budget director of the Office of Management and Budget, Jim Brigham, and my former Corporation Counsel, Allen Schwartz, who had already left government, becomes relevant.

As Allen said to Jim, "Very few people entering government leave with their reputations intact, and fewer still leave with their reputations enhanced." He was referring to newspaper articles and editorials adverse to high-level government personnel, seeking to convey the idea that while they were not criminals, they were close to it or otherwise unethical.

These two men, Allen and Jim, were two of the finest public

servants ever to have served, and their reputations based on their integrity were impeccable. They loved public service and each had served the city brilliantly, but each felt he was always walking on a high wire, with the press hoping they would fall during their tenure. It was nothing personal, just the desire of the media to feed the appetites of the public, who believes that many of their elected officials are probably crooks. The media in fact loved Brigham, Schwartz, and me.

I came through the corruption crises that plagued this city when Queens Borough President Donald Manes and Bronx County Leader Stanley Friedman were accused of corruption against the city government. Many people wondered how it could have happened in my administration. Because many people saw me as such a strong personality, some surely thought, "He had to or should have known." But I didn't, and I pointed out that the five district attorneys didn't know either. Neither did the two U.S. Attorneys, nor the Commissioner of Investigation. The criminality was picked up in a taped telephone conversation in Chicago. Manes subsequently committed suicide and Friedman went to prison. He served almost five years.

I was never seen as involved and, of course, I wasn't. I believe it is fair to say that I left city government with my reputation enhanced, as did Brigham and Schwartz.

In the November 2006 elections, I have no doubt that a number of U.S. Congressmen lost their seats because they were believed to be corrupt—some because they failed to pursue Congressman Mark Foley, who the world correctly saw as an abuser of young male Congressional pages, and others who were tied to corrupt lobbyists like Jack Abramoff.

Intellectual Honesty

I have said repeatedly, I believe in only one standard. It's either right or it's wrong. If it's right, then everybody has to be condemned if they're not doing it. I'm talking about standards of morality. As you begin your own path to create buzz, intellectual and financial honesty are important whether you're job hunting, campaigning, marketing a new product, starting a business—you name it. How honest are you being about your business, your product, your experience or campaign finances?

Early in my career I concluded that those coming in contact with me were impressed with my candor and honesty intellectually and financially. That's one of the ways buzz happened for me. Sure, sometimes I upset others in the process. But it was worth it. I told the press when I was mayor that there were at least two exceptions to my rule. I believed that when I fired someone who simply wasn't up to the job, I could say the person had quit and was not fired so as not to injure their reputation. That of course didn't apply if the individual was fired for dishonesty. In that case, the true reason had to be stated. I also believe you are not required to answer every reporter's question, and, although it is typically frowned upon, you can respond with a "no comment."

You can create buzz *if you are seen as willing to sacrifice a goal in pursuit of intellectual honesty. Intellectual honesty is when you say what you believe in even if it's not helpful to your cause. Such a person does get high marks. You may not win the campaign but, ultimately, you will win.*

The war on terrorism is a perfect example. I voted for President George W. Bush in the 2004 election because of the one issue that I believe trumped everything else: international terrorism. I had never before supported a Republican for president, but in my opinion, the candidate of the Democratic Party did not have the resoluteness to stand up to the terrorists. And as I've said over and over again: Bush, on this issue, has kept his word.

One September day during the 2004 presidential elections, I appeared on CNN's *American Morning* program to promote my first children's book, *Eddie: Harold's Little Brother*. During the interview, Bill Hemmer asked me a few questions about why I supported President Bush.

HEMMER: Let's talk about what happened at the convention. Longtime Democrat, you live down in Greenwich Village, for crying out loud.

KOCH: Yes, sure.

HEMMER: You ran this town for twelve years.

KOCH: Right.

HEMMER: And you're supporting George Bush. Why?

KOCH: I am for the simple reason that I believe his position in fighting international terrorism trumps all other issues. I don't agree with the president on a single domestic issue. But I believe the Democratic Party and Kerry don't have the stomach to take on international terrorism. I'm not attacking Kerry's patriotism. I'm attacking his philosophy.

And I believe that the most important issue—and when you have a country like Spain, a country like the Philippines, submitting to the demands of terrorism, in one case Spain withdrawing its troops from Iraq, and in the other case the Philippines withdrawing their civilian people from Iraq—you can see what terrorism, if it's unchecked, if it's not defeated, will do.

And the president's doctrine, the Bush doctrine of "We'll go after the terrorists and the countries that harbor them," I think is the right way to go. And the Democrats can't do it.

HEMMER: At the very beginning of your statement you said Kerry doesn't have the stomach.

KOCH: Yes.

HEMMER: What do you mean, the stomach?

KOCH: Well, the Democrats . . .

HEMMER: He doesn't have the guts? What does that mean?

KOCH: No, it has nothing to do with guts. It has to do with philosophy. I'm not attacking his guts, his patriotism, or his courage. But the people who are in charge of the Democratic Party today are his base. And, in fact, he's going back to his base.

There was a time when he said oh, yes, the war is the right thing to do. We're safer because Saddam Hussein is in prison, and all of the things that he should be saying. But now he's saying what the Deaniacs, so-called, have demanded: let's get out. And I believe that he is a prisoner, in a sense, of his base.

He has decided that trying to woo the middle class—which he tried to do—hasn't worked, because they don't believe him, and they're right not to believe him. And therefore, he's going back to his base to try to strengthen that.

HEMMER: Let's get to the book. It's called *Eddie*. What do we learn about you in this book?

KOCH: Well, it's a book that describes my brother and myself and our relationship. He was a great athlete. I was a terrible athlete. I had no coordination. But I wanted to play. And every year the team wanted my brother, Harold, on the team. They didn't want me. But Harold, my brother, said, if you want me, you've got to take Eddie. And that went on for some time.

And then one day my brother said, "Eddie, I can't do it any-more, you're no good." I said, "Harold, I want to play." He said, "You're no good and I can't do it." "What should I do, Harold?" "Do something you do good." 'What do I do good, Harold?' "You talk good." And that's what put me on the road to politics.

HEMMER: Lesson learned. Thank you. Good to see you, Ed Koch.

KOCH: Thank you.

Financial Honesty

I am a millionaire, all self-made since leaving public office. Gratefully, I will never have to worry about my ability to support myself, even if I lose all of my jobs with the passage of time—and I do not expect that to happen.

As I wrote in my book, *Politics*, when I was elected to Congress in 1968, I filed with the Clerk of the House of Representatives a statement of my net worth, and subsequently each year that I was in Congress I filed a new net worth statement and a complete copy of my federal tax return. My net worth at that time, including the surrender value of my life insurance policy, was $60,000. I did the same as mayor.

When I became mayor, because I believed in the growth of the U.S. economy, I invested all of my earnings each year from my salary and the books I wrote in the stock market. I've never stopped doing that in the seventeen years since I've been out of public office. And I never invested without the advice of a professional money manager.

So today I am independently wealthy, and I plan to leave my estate, which is less than $10 million but growing, to my seven grandnieces and grandnephews, all the grandchildren of my sister Pat and brother-in-law Alvin Thaler.

I am grateful for the wealth I have been able to accumulate over the years, and I have benefited educationally and professionally from holding office—but never financially. Of course, when I wrote books while I was mayor, people undoubtedly bought them because they were interested in my views as mayor. My honesty has kept me free of money scandals that some other politicians face through the choices they have made.

Remain Honest in All Situations

I decided long ago that the truth was powerful and strong—creating buzz was its aftermath. I realized that people sensed honesty and truth in others. As Merlin said to Arthur, in the movie *Excalibur,* "When a man lies, he murders some part of the world." It's true. Every lie you tell affects not only the listener, but you. It is a slippery slope.

Being dishonest, *intellectually or financially, is like carrying a secret burden. Ultimately, you should be found out—and you often are—and pay a heavy price.*

How can you seek to be honest in your statements all the time? Simple. Most lies are for the purpose of covering up mistakes. One must come to the conclusion that you are strengthened, particularly in politics, by admitting error, rather than engaging in a cover-up, which when uncovered is always worse in the minds of others than the original error. Just ask Bill Clinton.

Honesty can cause conflict. The kind that is gut-wrenching, upsetting, and confrontational with people. But I was not and never will be afraid of controversy. And neither should you be. You just need to be good at presenting your best case, in a forthright fashion. If you avoid the truth, you will likely be found out and fail, if not immediately, then at a later date.

One of my mottos *on my City Hall desk during the twelve years that I was mayor was the title of a Catholic hymn I heard* *sung at the Christmas midnight masses I attended—and which I still do attend—at Saint Patrick's Cathedral. That hymn is "Be Not Afraid." I love the melody and the words. I am Jewish, not Catholic, but I am moved by the spirit displayed by my Catholic friends taking communion. Have no fear, I've no desire to convert. I am proud of my Jewish heritage and religion.*

Here are the two main rules to follow when you find yourself in conflict with someone:

Rule #1: *Listen well.* Interruptions block the flow of communication and prevent progress. Sometimes an interruption jars or upsets the speaker. Give people your attention. Let them finish their explanations and thoughts. Do your best to understand what they're saying. You don't have to agree with what they're saying, but try to understand it from their point of view: Try to understand why they think that way. And *let them know* you understand.

Rule #2: *Try to speak only what's strictly true.* This sounds a lot easier than it is. Try it. Just try going a single day saying only what you know is true. It's tougher than you'd think, so don't treat this one lightly.

If you compel yourself to follow these simple disciplines, you'll have more control over the direction you want to take. This is no small accomplishment. To some, honesty may sound old-fashioned, but I assure you that honesty means more buzz.

Of course, it is certainly true that almost everyone lies or exaggerates on some occasions. But realize that your credibility is affected when that lie is detected at a later time. Lying under oath is a criminal matter and is never acceptable under any circumstances.

Chapter Two

FINDING YOUR NICHE

I created a slogan that has identified me for almost forty years, and it is as well known today by New Yorkers as it was years ago. That slogan is "How'm I doing?" It cost nothing to create.

When I was a congressman, every Friday morning at 7 A.M. I would go to a major subway station or bus stop and hand out literature consisting of statements I had made that week in Congress or on issues that editorial writers were discussing. (In those days the Congress rarely met on Fridays.) The statements might be about domestic issues, such as affordable housing, or foreign affairs, such as the U.S. involvement in the Mideast and particularly with Israel.

Initially, at the stops I would offer the literature and say, "I'm Ed Koch." Before I could finish speaking and hand them the paper, they would rush by me, obviously viewing me as an obstacle in their path.

Some of the backgound information for this chapter was obtained in an interview of Chloe Z. Clark, Ph.D., Columbia University, Career Rainbow, LLC.

One day I began saying to the subway passengers, "I'm Ed Koch, your congressman. How'm I doing?" On almost every occasion, people would stop. I think they thought, "What a novel idea. I'll tell him." And they did. Most of the comments were favorable, a few not so favorable, and some very unfavorable. I knew I was on to something. I had involved them by asking for their opinion.

From that day on, I used that phrase and it worked. Not only did people stop to offer their opinions, they accepted my handouts. In the handout I often asked that they write a letter to a state or federal official to advance a particular proposal, and to send me a copy of their letter. When I received copies of the many letters that were sent, I would add the individuals' names to my mailing list. Today it would be an e-mail list, but long ago it was snail mail.

No one could have a better relationship than I have had with the voters who knew me as their councilman, congressman, and mayor. I respected them and they returned my affection for them many times over.

There have been a few people over the years who responded to my question negatively. When that happened, I engaged them in intense conversation and tried to dissuade them from their opinions. I treated them respectfully, if they were not rude. If they were rude, I would respond with a put-down, or I sometimes appealed to onlookers to "vote" on the issue, indicating whether they agreed with me or the heckler.

I like to think my slogan, which came to identify me in the minds of many people, is one of the best—not only in the political world, but also in the business world or even in everyday life. Although I left public office seventeen years ago hardly a day goes by without someone smiling on seeing me on the street and saying to me, "How'm I doing?" I always respond, generally with, "You are, I'm sure, doing fine. How about me?" Their response is usually, "Fine." Sometimes I will even have people from across the street yelling to me, "Don't ask. You're doing fine."

I know I'm lucky. Corporations spend billions of dollars developing slogans and marketing campaigns to sell company products and become known. *Advertising Age*, the New York-based weekly trade publication covering the advertising industry, published on their website in the Fall of 2006 that the top 100 companies in this country spent almost $102 billion in 2005 on advertising expenses to market the brands they manufacture.

While I do not consider myself a brand, I do have brand appeal. I believe there is awareness of my name and face not only throughout the United States, but also in Europe and Japan. That probably stems from my having been mayor for three terms and having traveled a lot and being known for my comments here in the United States and abroad. When I was mayor, I made it a point to travel internationally at least once a year. New York City—under every mayor—has conducted its own foreign policy. My press conferences with leaders around the world enhanced my reputation and buzz.

I was famous for my outspokenness in chiding other countries, such as England on her Ireland policies, or criticizing Daniel Ortega and the Sandinistas after first helping them when I was a congressman when they opposed Somoza in Nicaragua. I attacked China for its savagery in Tiananmen Square and placed a street sign at a corner next to the Chinese mission on the west side of Manhattan, calling the corner Tiananmen Square, infuriating the Chinese. I constantly criticized the United Nations for its hostility to Israel, calling it a "cesspool" and a "monument to hypocrisy."

Get to Know Yourself

In *Poor Richard's Almanack*, Benjamin Franklin wrote that three of the hardest things in the world are diamonds, steel, and knowing yourself. I would agree. I believe that I know myself. I know I'm a worrier—a Jewish syndrome. I also know I am resolute and will do what has to be done. I never ask staff to communicate a tough message; I do it directly.

Speaking in front of an audience has always been my forte. I found my niche—though I wasn't aware at the time where I would end up professionally—when I wasn't allowed to play anymore with my older brother Harold's baseball team as a young boy.

As a result, I knew my niche would always involve public speaking. Plus, I wanted to do something that would give something back to the City of New York for all it has done for me and my immigrant parents. I never mapped out a ten-year time frame to become mayor, but once I heard politicians speak, such as Adlai Stevenson in 1952, I was off and running. Stevenson was a phenomenal writer and speaker. Yet although I campaigned for him, I would not be like Stevenson—he was a patrician and more rhetoric than action, and I was just a Jewish kid born in the Bronx.

I have always perceived myself as representing middle-class values. My campaigns were therefore directed at the middle class. Every ethnic and racial group in New York City—blacks, Hispanics, whites, Asians—all aspire to be middle class. My critics often foolishly referred to me as the "middle-class mayor," thinking that was derisive and would hurt me. How wrong they were. I gloried in it.

Harry Truman, the 33rd president of the United States, was another person whom I greatly admired and still do. Truman was an ordinary guy and dealt with the people of this country in a straightforward, common-sense way. Fiorello LaGuardia, another person who had an impact on my life, was a fellow New Yorker whom every mayor respected. He and I both weathered very difficult financial crises suffered by the city while each of us was mayor.

So, sometimes finding your niche means recognizing which mentors or people to whom you are drawn you want to emulate. You may not end up doing exactly what they do, as we each have our own unique talents and gifts, but you can determine your niche certainly by trying and learning.

Why find your niche? Because once you know yourself well enough to know your talents and skills, you are that much closer to creating buzz. You want to capture the attention of voters, consumers, or the media to the point where talking about you becomes an integral, entertaining, fascinating, and newsworthy part of their day. Creating buzz is about starting conversations, and you want the conversation to focus on you; when appropriate.

But if you don't utilize your talent, you're going to end up not finding your niche and possibly hating your job. I always tell college students and those just starting out in their jobs, "If you don't really like what you are doing, quit now before your obligations—family, mortgage, and children, in particular—make it too difficult to give up your income. Being happy in your work is equally important as being happy in your home life."

Finding your niche requires you to think realistically about yourself—your talents, skills, and interests. Don't think, "I want the best job tomorrow." Think about what you want to be accomplishing five to ten years out. People get stuck, hopping from one job to another rather than planning a career track. If you do job hop, ask yourself how the particular job is going to fit into your overall idea of the direction you are seeking. Sometimes there are financial considerations, and you end up taking the job that pays the most money or that is available right now, but when you get to the point where that financial burden eases off a little, look at the jobs that will help you realize long-term goals.

Dreams are important, too, especially when you are younger. What did you always dream about being? It's a simplistic example, but let's say you wanted to be an astronaut. Although that's probably not a real possibility, as you get older you can still find a career that somehow interacts with astronauts or the space

SOME TOOLS TO HELP YOU FIND YOUR NICHE

You can find your niche by performing a self-assessment that will get you from A to Z in your career path. Many career assessment tests look at your skills, your talents, your interests, and your experiences. Some tests really help you in doing a self-evaluation or choosing what you need from your environment in order to be more productive on the job. For example:

The *Campbell Interest and Skill Survey,* also known as CISS, uses targeted questions to help you understand how you fit in the working world. This 320-question test not only looks at what you are interested in, but it enables you to evaluate yourself in terms of what you think your skills are.

The *Birkman* is a test that identifies key strengths and motivations, and what you need from your environment in order to be most productive on the job. So you can have a job as a bookkeeper, for example, but if it isn't in an environment suited to who you are and where you best operate, no matter how much you love the work, the environment isn't going to give you what you need and will therefore thwart your potential success.

Myers-Briggs is less of a career-assessment test and more of a personality exam, which career counselors use to help clients find their niche. It is often mentioned because of its reputation as a solid tool that has helped many people.

There are many other tests career counselors use to help people find their niche. Each offers suggestions or answers to help point out different directions and give people a different way of thinking about themselves.

program. Very few of us plan a career that is related to something we've always wanted to do. Incorporate the dreams you had when you were younger into the work you are doing now.

Knowing what you're passionate about *is just as important as understanding your strengths. And determining where the two intersect is even more important. Create a list of the things you are passionate about and another list of those things you are good at doing. Looking over both lists, select those items that can generate income.*

In addition to my passion for speaking, what I like best about all my activities is the ability to educate others on matters in which I believe I have an expertise. I do that with my weekly written Commentaries, which are sent out by e-mail to more than 1,000 recipients, many of them in the media. Many of those people to whom I send my Commentaries write back to me, often agreeing and stating they thought so well of the Commentary that they sent it on to their own mailing lists. I like to think of myself as an educator, so I am always providing information and not waiting to be asked. This supports my point that yes, buzz is self-propelling, but it requires constant restarting and reinforcement.

Marketing Yourself

Sometimes finding your niche comes in the form of a job interview. Think of yourself as a product—you are putting yourself out there in the marketplace. Questions to ask yourself include:

- What are your strengths?
- What do you bring to the table that is special?
- How can this help you and/or the company?

Finding your niche in this situation is not about you—it is about them. Identify what the company needs and position yourself from the perspective of the company. For me, on my first day in office as mayor, running this city was not about me—it was about the people and what they needed. I announced I would need three terms—12 years—to solve the city's problems. When I left, I could proudly point to a number of major accomplishments, which I describe in detail in Chapter 6.

So many people go into a job process thinking about what it is *they* need or want. That is understandable. But, if you are talking about a marketplace, if you are talking about selling yourself and making a name for yourself, then your approach should be based on what you can do for them. When you find your niche and know what is unique about you, you can then present it in the best way possible so that employers—or voters—can see it also.

You must show prospective employers how you can make profits higher and costs lower. Tell them, "You don't have to do it on your own, I can really help you out with this"—but mean what you say. If you have a wealth of experience, say so, and let them know how you can put this wealth of experience to work for them.

If you are in a situation where your firm is downsizing employees and you've lost your job—and most of us have been there—it is a challenge. The way to survive is to control your thinking. If you are older and have a vast amount of experience under your belt, exhibit it and use it. American society does not value older adults enough, and many older adults do not value themselves enough either. Quite often they do not see the assets they are bringing to the situation. A sense of who you are without arrogance or hubris is essential. Most skills employees learn

Do you find yourself muttering any of the following in your head?

- I've never been happy in my job. Maybe I should look elsewhere.
- What if I find my dream job and I'm still dissatisfied?
- How will I explain it to people?
- Maybe I should stop worrying about my calling and get a real job.

I don't believe in self-flagellation. Accept and recognize reality and the need to improve on what you're doing.

If you have a negative view of your talents, seek to improve them through education. If you are really talented but still negative about yourself, get professional help.

in their jobs can be transferred to and utilized in other careers. Everything you learn is useful—especially if you learn to do it well.

When making a transition, people can get lost in a fog of uncertainty. Sometimes depression sets in and a lack of self-worth surfaces. It's so easy for us to take what other people say about us as the truth, even though it isn't. Keep in mind that when you are discovering your niche, no matter what your lot in life, put more objectivity on the table and shed more light on your assets. That's where an assessment test may help verify what you already know about yourself.

When I lost my election for fourth term as mayor, I honestly felt free and believed that my life had been extended. I thought if I had been reelected I would have died in office. I knew I would be okay in the private sector. I became a partner in a law firm, now called Bryan Cave, LLP, I wrote columns for newspapers, and I got a radio show and a television program. I became a motivational speaker for hire. I was immediately successful, as I am today. My earlier prophecy, "If all the people I've irritated got together, you could throw me out"—as they did— "and I'll get a better job and you won't get a better mayor" came true only financially. There is no better job than mayor.

While all of us can do better, given a second chance, I nevertheless would basically do what I did all over again if I had to be mayor again today.

Above all, do not be afraid to be yourself. That's the quickest way to discover your niche. There is no one quite like you, and you'll have a better chance of appealing to most people if you are yourself. I don't mind walking alone. Others may not like it, but this is what I'm doing. Do what you feel comfortable with, not what others expect you to do.

Chapter Three

THE POWER OF MY PEN

One sure-fire way to create buzz is through your correspondence.

When you write to officials, executives, or other well-known people to commend them for something they have done or to take them to task for something you don't agree with, you keep your name out there as someone with something to say. When you answer the correspondence of those who contact you, especially people who are not well known, you show that you are interested in hearing what everybody has to say on a given subject.

Writing letters began for me when I was elected to Congress. I had a rule that every letter I received had to receive a substantive reply from the office staff within two weeks. As I recall, the office received thousands of letters in some weeks, so the replies had to be brief. Many people who wrote raised a number of topics in their letters. My way to deal with the letters to which I personally responded was to select the most important or interesting issue they raised and give it prime attention, responding briefly or not at all to the other, lesser issues.

Every day my chief of staff, Diane Coffey, would give me up to twenty letters to which I would personally respond. My staff prepared responses to the other letters. In addition, every morning I would select about ten letters from the mail bag, lottery fashion, and read them to ascertain what was on the minds of the constituents in my district, known as the 17th "Silk Stocking District." It was the Gold Coast because of the wealth of the people living there. I once reported that the concerns of the district's residents, conveyed by their letters, were "Save the Whales"; "Save the Dolphins"; and "Save the Jews"—in that order of priority.

I knew the shorter the letter, the better, and through practice I learned to make every sentence count. I knew I would never be as good at it as Bill Buckley, who set the gold standard for letter writing. The letters included in this book were written for different purposes, which I will now try to explain.

Randi Weingarten

My letter to Randi Weingarten, president of the United Federation of Teachers (UFT), was to have the expertise of the teachers in that union, who felt threatened by the concept of charter schools competing with public schools, used to develop a new type of school that would better educate our children. I wanted the UFT to lessen and, if possible, end its opposition to the changes, to support the charter school movement, and to support the removal of union-imposed restrictions that hindered teaching and learning in the public schools. To accomplish that I believed the UFT had to be part of the charter school movement, and my letter was intended to entice them in.

Randi did exactly what I proposed and opened a charter school in Brooklyn. In fact, while she did not reply in writing, she did call me. She was so proud of the accomplishments of the UFT charter school that she invited me to be a part of a documentary she had made in the school, which I was honored to do.

Pat Robertson

The letter I wrote to Reverend Robertson was sent because he shares my belief that it is in the interest of the U.S. to support the State of Israel, particularly its security. We share a common belief that Islamic terrorism is a threat to western civilization and that the only real ally in the Mideast that the U.S. can count on is the State of Israel.

Robertson, an acknowledged conservative, has been attacked by many politically involved citizens for his positions on a number of domestic issues. He has been attacked by a number of Jewish citizens who are liberals and totally opposed to his conservative agenda. I wanted him to know that there are liberal Jews who appreciated his efforts and statements concerning Israel. If someone is providing substantial support to Israel and leading his constituency to do the same, and all he ever gets are brickbats from Jewish supporters of Israel, he may tire in his efforts and constancy. I did not want that to happen. A little appreciation goes a long way.

Edward I. Koch

1290 Avenue of the Americas
30th Floor
New York, New York 10104

Tel: (212) 541-2100
Fax: (212) 541-1321
E-Mail: eikoch@bryancave.com

February 17, 2004

Randi Weingarten
President
United Federation of Teachers
52 Broadway
New York, New York 10004

Dear Randi:

It is disheartening for all of us who are concerned about the poor state of education in the City's school system to witness the sometimes savage attacks exchanged between you and the Chancellor. You and Joel are both dedicated, able and superb public servants and I have no doubt that both of you have the education of the City's children as your first priority.

In collective bargaining, you each have different roles with you representing teachers (employees) and he representing management (Mayor and the City). There, understandably, the relationship is adversarial, but there are many areas relating to education outside of collective bargaining where you and he should be working together. I have a suggestion.

Why doesn't the U.F.T. request of the Chancellor the opportunity to operate at least five elementary and five high schools as charter schools. Those schools selected should be currently on the failing schools list. When you and your colleagues are in charge of those schools, you can set the curriculum, rules and regulations, as do the other charter schools. If you are right and by using your educational procedures, substantially upgrade the education of the children in those schools, you will have established for the Chancellor and the people of the City that the Chancellor should have listened to your proposals long ago. I have no doubt that if you make such a proposal to the Chancellor, he will accede to it. If I can be of assistance, please let me know.

All the best.

Sincerely,

Edward I. Koch

Edward I. Koch

1290 Avenue of the Americas
30th Floor
New York, New York   10104

Tel: (212) 541-2100
Fax: (212) 541-1321
E-Mail: eikoch@bryancave.com

January 28, 2004

Reverend Pat Robertson
CBN World Headquarters
977 Centerville Turnpike,
Virginia Beach, Virginia, 23463

Dear Reverend Robertson:

I was recently told of your address to the Herzliya Conference on December 17th by Norman Podhoretz who, as you know, is a brilliant writer, dedicated to the survival of the Jewish people, and a good friend. I secured a copy of your speech, "Why Evangelical Christians Support Israel," from your website.

Your support of Israel has been marvelous to behold and extremely important to the Jewish nation. I want to thank you for your latest remarks which again provide support at this moment when the world is so bent on the destruction of the Jewish nation.

I am enclosing my most recent commentary on the U.S. invasion of Iraq. I believe that President Bush deserves reelection for his dedication to the destruction of terrorists and the countries that harbor them, and I am voting for him. It will be the first time that I have voted for a Republican for president.

I have taken the liberty of adding your name to my e-mail list, so you will be receiving my weekly commentaries.

All the best and, again, many thanks.

Sincerely,

Edward I. Koch

Enclosure

ıe Christian Broadcasting
Network, Inc.

Pat Robertson
Chairman of the Board and
Chief Executive Officer

M. G. "Pat" Robertson
977 Centerville Turnpike, SHB-301
Virginia Beach, VA 23463
Private contacts:
24/7 phone: 757/226-2778
FAX: 757/226-2775
E-mail: ggconklin@erols.com

February 3, 2004

The Honorable Edward I. Koch
1290 Avenue of the Americas
30th Floor
New York, NY 10104

Dear Ed:

Thank you for your gracious letter. You have always been someone who I regard as very special. To this day I think of you as the "great Mayor of New York," and I am deeply grateful for your service to our nation.

It has been my privilege to be a friend and supporter of Israel, and I am happy that over the years I have been able to speak out in support of the cause in which I so very passionately believe. Your remarks concerning the President and Israel are excellent and something that could be very helpful to the President in this very hotly contested election coming up next Fall.

I would enjoy receiving more of your commentaries on various issues. It is always a pleasure to hear from you.

With warm personal regards, I remain…

Cordially yours,

Pat Robertson
Chairman of the Board and
Chief Executive Officer

PR:ggc

A Political Attack

In dealing with offensive anonymous letters, I sometimes use a time-honored response first issued by U.S. Senator Stephen Young, a Democrat from Ohio, many years ago, giving it a modern update. Senator Young's exact words were: "Some crackpot has written to me and signed your name to the letter. I thought you ought to know about this before it gets any further."

Joseph Bruno

My letter to Joe Bruno, majority leader of the New York Senate, was intended to thank him for his help in securing legislation providing state-wide protection against discrimination to gay and lesbian New Yorkers in the private sector. He evidently appreciated my acknowledgment of his good deed.

November 24, 2005

Ed Koch
Bryan Cave Robinson Silverman
1290 Avenue of the Americas
New York, NY 10104

Mr. Koch:

In the midst of the 2004 presidential campaign I [got] a piece of political propaganda (AKA trash) from you, supporting the liar in the White House and I want to say to you that

I AM DEEPLY OFFENDED!

Was it <u>you</u> who sat down with a telephone book and picked out names:

"Oh, look, here's a **_Jew_** name, let's send a letter to him."

This is what I instruct you to do for me:

1. **REMOVE** my name from your mailing list,
2. **NEVER** communicate with me ever again in any form,
3. **ATTEMPT** to find _reputable_ and _honest_ political candidates to support.
4. **KEEP** your political biases to yourself. Your opinions stink.

Do not respond to this letter. I don't want your _trash_ in my mailbox.

Edward I. Koch

1290 Avenue of the Americas
37th Floor
New York, New York 10104

Tel: (212) 541-2100
Fax: (212) 541-1321
E-Mail: eikoch@bryancave.com

November 29, 2005

Dear

    Some fool apparently signed your name to a letter which was sent to me. I bring it to your attention to alert you to the possibility that you have been the victim of identity theft.

    All the best.

Sincerely,

Edward I. Koch

Edward I. Koch

1290 Avenue of the Americas
30th Floor
New York, New York 10104

Tel. (212) 541-2100
Fax: (212) 541-1321
E-Mail: eikoch@bryancave.com

December 24, 2002

The Honorable Joseph L. Bruno
Majority Leader
New York State Senate
The Capitol
Albany, New York 12247

Dear Joe:

Over the years, we have discussed passage of the gay rights legislation. When you told me that your caucus opposed it and would not permit the bill to be brought to the floor for a vote, I must confess I did not believe that could be possible. Yet, events established it was true, and it took your major efforts to secure the 13 Republican votes that ultimately were cast in support of the legislation.

It would not have happened without you, and I hope that supporters of the legislation -- in and out of the Legislature, Democrats and Republicans -- give you full credit.

If any of the 13 Republican Senators find themselves in difficulty in their next election as a result of their vote in favor of the bill, I would be happy to issue a statement defending them on this issue. When I was mayor and similar legislation was before the City Council, I made the same commitment to members, irrespective of their political affiliation, who wanted to vote for it but were afraid of the political consequences. None of them found themselves in any danger in their next election because of their vote, and none needed my help. I suspect that will be the case for your members who voted for the legislation.

In any event, I want to congratulate you on your leadership and courage.

All the best.

Sincerely,

Edward I. Koch

THE SENATE
STATE OF NEW YORK
ALBANY 12247

JOSEPH L. BRUNO
PRESIDENT PRO TEM

MAJORITY LEADER

(518) 455-3191

January 2, 2003

Mr. Edward I. Koch
1290 Avenue of the Americas
30th Floor
New York, New York 10104

Dear Ed:

Thank you for your very encouraging letter, and for all of the support that you have given the Republican Majority in the past. I am glad that we were able to recognize the importance of the gay rights legislation. It is unfortunate that it took so long to pass, but at least it is done now.

The issue of gay rights is one which people often relate to politically, rather than objectively. You have been a staunch advocate for equality and anti-discrimination, which is very much a credit to you in your life.

Thank you again for all of the support that you have given me and my Conference. I look forward to staying in touch.

Sincerely,

Joseph L. Bruno

JLB:acl

Nasty E-Mail

Each week I send Commentaries by e-mail to a large number of people, many of whom I have never met. E-mail is God's gift to people like me who like to write and have their opinions read by others without having to spend prohibitive postage costs. In case you want to be added to my e-mail list to receive my Commentaries, the address is eikoch@bryancave.com.

Below are two examples of e-mails I received in response to my Commentaries. I answered them both, and to a limited extent the writer of the second, disgraceful e-mail apologized.

E-Mail Correspondence

E-Mail Received from Reader

Dear Ed:

I had the pleasure of watching your recent interview with Cavuto on the Fox network. Encouraging war with Iran? Good move, lets get this Armageddon party going !!!

Hey, are you sure you're a Democrat ? Because you make Bush, Cheney, Rove and all the neocon crooks and cronies proud with your rhetoric.

Nuke ya ! Nuke ya !

Have a nice day,

Ed Koch Replies

I'm sorry you don't agree. The Iranian government has called the U.S. the "great Satan" for years, and both the U.S. and Israel have been assailed and threatened. In the past our embassy personnel were held hostage in Iran for more than a year. If Iran threatens us with a nuclear bomb, should we wait until the nuclear bomb arrives by rocket or in a terrorist's luggage before responding appropriately?

Notwithstanding your attempt at humor, I am a proud Democrat and a liberal with both sanity and common sense.

All the best.
Ed Koch

E-Mail Received from Reader

Mr. Koch,

In The Right Man *author David Frum explains why fellow neoconservatives (aka Jewish-Americans) support Bush: "Why did the Republican Party become Zionist? Certainly the influence of evangelical Christians has a lot to do with it. Many evangelicals identify the return of the Jews to Israel as a sign of the imminence of the Second Coming—and see the attacks on Israel as portending the Antichrist." Ergo, Saddam sponsored Palestinian suicide attacks against Israel; Saddam was the Antichrist.*

I respect your right as a Jew to lobby for the security of Isreal [sic]. However, evangelical conservative Christians are very strange bedfellows for a Jewish gay man who has no other shared values other than a flawed Isreali-centric Middle East policy. Saddam was a real and present threat to Isreal, there is no evidence that he (a secular dictator) was a threat to the United States (for as long as he was contained by our forces under several United Nations' mandates).

The US and Isreal are at war with Muslim extremists. Muslim extremists have been emboldened by the occupation of Iraq by a predominantly Christian army. Prior to the invasion of Iraq the US was respected by most Arab countries (whereas the Europeans were disliked for their transgressions as colonial powers). Today the US is the most despised nation on the planet. Accordingly, the majority of Americans realize the occupation of a Muslim country has increased the probability of more terrorist attacks against the homeland.

When (not if) the next atrocity against the US by Jihadists occurs, critics of the war will remember those responsible: Wolfowitz, Feith, Libby, Abrams, Podhoretz, Perle, Kristol, Krauthammer, Miller, and other neoconservatives. Please do not destroy your legacy by supporting a misadventure that will inevitably result in a civil war and the Iraqi Shiites united with Iran against Isreal.

Ed Koch Replies

Your letter could have been written by Pat Buchanan. You may remember that he blamed the Jews for Gulf War I with his "Amen Corner" litany, as you blame them for Gulf War II. The position that both of you take is in a way similar to the thesis of the Protocols of Zion (a forgery), which is that Jews historically manipulate those who are in charge of government.

So here, referring now to Gulf War II, President Bush, Vice President Dick Cheney, Secretary of Defense Donald Rumsfeld, Secretary of State Colin Powell, National Security Advisor Condoleezza Rice and CIA Director George Tenet, all of whom supported the war with Iraq, in your opinion, were brainwashed by neocon Jews and got us into war, and that these leaders did not act as a result of their own decisions and independent wills.

Your reference to my alleged sexuality is disgraceful as well as irrelevant even to your thesis, unless you believe that the Gulf War is the result of a gay conspiracy. Regrettably, such allusions are not uncommon from people with your anti-Semitic views. I have found over the years that people who gratuitously characterize someone else's sexuality without having any knowledge on the subject, or any basis for doing so, it being in any event irrelevant to the discussion at hand, often fall into either of two categories: repressed homosexuals frightened that they may be gay or homophobes who are often mentally unstable.

If you are in the first category, don't be fearful. Remember, I am responsible for a New York City law prohibiting discrimination against anyone on the basis of their sexual orientation, including transvestites. If you are in the second, I suggest that you consult a qualified mental health professional.

Happy Thanksgiving.
Ed Koch

Response from Reader

Mr. Koch,

I apologize for characterizing you as a Jewish gay man. Obviously your sexual orientation is irrelevant to the contribution that you have made to society. My intent was to illustrate the deep divide between evangelical Christian's intolerance and the Jewish tradition of fighting for the civil rights of all Americans.

Bob Woodward's Plan of Attack *makes clear President Bush came into office intent on removing Saddam. Wolfowitz and Company wrote an open letter in the*

*1990s to President Clinton demanding the removal of
Saddam from power.*

*Prior to the mid-term elections in 2002 the American
people had changed their focus from the successful route
of the Taliban in Afghanistan to corruption in the board
room, losses in the stock market (blamed on others), loss
of jobs, etc. Ergo, the Republican Party was in trouble.
Rove understood that the key to a successful mid-term
election was to sell the need for a strong Commander-In-
Chief and exploit the perception that the Democrats are
weak on defense. Strong CIC's are needed during wars,
or when the country is threatened by another country (not
a rag-tag bunch of Jihadists). Secondly, the Bush Base saw
Saddam as the anti-Christ. Thirdly, the neocons wanted
to defeat the primary threat to Isreal [sic]. The three
separate and independent forces of Rove, evangelicals,
and neocons formed the perfect storm and the Democrats
failed in their responsibility as the loyal opposition. I hold
Kerry and Company equally responsible (especially
knowing that LBJ had taken the country to war in a very
similar fashion).*

*Within the next few years there will be a civil war in
Iraq. The majority Shiites will form an alliance with Iran
in reaction to the support the Sunnis will receive from
Syria and the Saudis. The responsibility for the consequences will be with those who supported the invasion.*

Ed Koch Replies

*You haven't apologized for your anti-Semitic
comment.*

All the best.
Ed Koch

Ray Kelly

My letter to police commissioner Ray Kelly was intended to reiterate executive orders I had issued protecting illegal immigrants when it came to their health, the education of their children, and reporting physical assaults upon them. I wanted to emphasize and defend the importance of those orders which were under attack.

Police Commissioner Kelly confirmed the policy of the New York City Police Department to be as follows:

- Not to inquire about any person's immigration status unless investigating activity other than mere status as an undocumented alien.
- To cooperate with federal authorities in investigating and apprehending aliens suspected of criminal activity.
- Not to inquire about the immigration status of crime victims, witnesses, or others who call or approach the police seeking assistance.

Saudi Arabian Delegation

In this final letter, sent to a member of the Saudi Arabian delegation in Washington, D.C., I was simply seeking to point out—and did so by making my letter public—the inconsistencies in the alleged Saudi support for the United States. Because the Saudis need us, they will help where they can, but I don't think they can be trusted.

Edward I. Koch

1290 Avenue of the Americas
37th Floor
New York, New York   10104

Tel: (212) 541-2100
Fax: (212) 541-1321.
E-Mail: eikoch@bryancave.com

February 10, 2004

Raymond W. Kelly
Police Commissioner
The City of New York
Police Department
One Police Plaza
New York, New York   10007

Dear Ray:

I am enclosing a copy of an article by Heather MacDonald which appeared in *City Journal* entitled, "The Illegal-Alien Crime Wave."

Ms. MacDonald comments on cities, including New York City, which have limited the turning in of aliens and information about them to the Immigration and Naturalization Service under certain circumstances.

When I was mayor, I initiated that policy with respect to the New York City Police Department arresting aliens. I thought the policy we established was not to arrest aliens who reported a crime committed against them or sought medical treatment unless the alien had committed some crime other than being in the United States illegally. On page 4 of her article, Ms. MacDonald writes that misdemeanors and even some felonies are now not a reason for notifying the INS and she goes on to attack Mayor Bloomberg's current policy as even worse than the earlier one.

Since I am called quite often on this issue and take pride in saying that I established the policy, I want to be certain that the policy I initiated has not changed since I left office or, if it has, to know what changes have been made.

I would appreciate knowing what the current policy is and your thoughts on the matter.

All the best and many thanks.

Sincerely,

Edward I. Koch

Enclosure

Edward I. Koch

1290 Avenue of the Americas
30th Floor
New York, New York 10104

Tel. (212) 541-2100
Fax: (212) 541-1321
E-Mail: eikoch@bryancave.com

December 4, 2002

Adel Al Jubeir
c/o Royal Embassy of Saudi Arabia
601 New Hampshire Avenue, N.W.
Washington, D.C. 20037

Dear Mr. Al Jubeir:

I understand and can sympathize with your distress that, after decades of good relations between our two countries, the relationship between Saudi Arabia and the United States as viewed by the American public has seriously deteriorated.

It may well be that the wife of the Saudi ambassador was tricked into making charitable contributions that ultimately ended up with two of the Sept. 11 hijackers. However, on the very same day that you announced that the Saudi kingdom has and is continuing to take measures to prevent support by Saudi citizens of Al Qaeda and other terrorist groups, Saudi Interior Minister Prince Naif Ibn Abd Al-Aziz is reported in today's New York Post as blaming Jews for the World Trade Center catastrophe "while denying involvement by any Saudi in the Sept. 11 attacks."

Surely, you know this to be a flagrant lie. Don't you believe it is essential, in order to establish the Kingdom's bona fides in seeking to repair relations between Saudi Arabia and the United States, that you denounce Prince Naif for these unmitigated falsehoods? I have seen you many times in the media, particularly on CNN, seeking to clear Saudi Arabia from any involvement in the Sept. 11 attacks. Unless you grasp the mettle and denounce fellow Saudis who attempt to fraudulently shift the blame to Jews -- which no rational person accepts -- all of your efforts will fail.

I do hope that you will respond.

All the best.

Sincerely,

Edward I. Koch

Of all the things that I do professionally, writing provides me with the greatest pleasure. I'm not a great writer, but I am a good one, and my writings contain my voice. During my mayoralty in 1984, I published a book titled *Mayor*, which sold 150,000 copies. During a press conference at City Hall an out-of-town reporter said to me, "Mr. Mayor, how do we know that you wrote this book?" I replied, "It's easy. Close your eyes and have someone read it to you and you will hear my voice."

I hope you hear my voice in this book as well.

Part Two

CREATING A STIR

In October of 2005, a group of prominent New York City journalists, novelists, columnists, clergy, and union workers held a panel discussion about my impact on New York City while I was mayor. This forum chat coincided with the launching of the exhibition, "New York City Comes Back: Ed Koch and the City," at the Museum of the City of New York.

Michael Goodwin, former *Daily News* editor and moderator of the panel, quipped to the panelists, "Mayor Koch was so in your face for so long that a whole generation of children grew up thinking 'Mayor' was his first name."

Since I have been in politics, the cost of campaigning has risen exponentially and with the speed of light. Campaigns even for relatively modest positions now involve millions of dollars. The most costly aspects of campaigns are television commercials. I believe that since the airwaves belong to the people, commercials during elections should be free time provided by the television stations. I don't know about political advertising today, but for the most part, politicians have paid the highest rates instead of the lowest rates.

When I started my political career, I was speaking for others, like Adlai Stevenson. The buzz I created was as a result of the debates that I engaged in from the top of the soapbox I stood on in the streets of Greenwich Village. The major location was the corner of 7th Avenue and 4th Street. If you do generate buzz and become practiced, people get to know you. When you set up your own open forum, people are happy, since they will have the chance to take you on. People simply like to do that. For a candidate, it's great practice.

Although money is important for commercials, becoming known doesn't necessarily require money. It does require getting around, doing things that are helpful to others.

Chapter Four

CRAFTING YOUR VISION

On April 20, 1981, Clyde Haberman of the *New York Times* wrote an article about me titled "The Koch Method for Winning Audiences and Influencing Voters," after watching me speak in front of 500 members at the lounge of the Yale Club a few nights before.

I remember that night well, but for me it was no more than a usual public-speaking engagement. The audience and I ping-ponged various questions, and I gave them my honest answers. We covered much material—from capital punishment, the dilapidated subways, and garbage littering the streets, to the other quality of life issues in New York. My remarks and the audience's response were very similar to many other engagements I've had over the years. Haberman, however, observed I was more "on" than usual; perhaps it was because I was gearing up for my reelection campaign. Also, I was doing what I love to do best—public speaking, entertaining, and embracing a crowd.

But what Haberman was able to do—and what I hope to do for you with this book—is capture my vision and how I follow through, whether it be in front of an audience or in day-to-day business. In essence, how I create my public buzz.

For public-speaking engagements, I share my vision and want to educate and motivate others. I may not always provide a direction, depending on the nature of the event. Sharing my vision, however, gives listeners something to believe in, work toward, and identify with.

My primary goal during my first term as mayor was to save the city from pending possible bankruptcy. There was nothing that I would permit to get in my way of making it happen.

First, I had to restructure the poverty programs and get the programs back on track so they would serve the poor and were not misused by the "poverty pimps" (an ill-conceived phrase, which I did not invent but did use in describing those who ripped off the programs). Many people opposed me and my administration's efforts. To put it bluntly, we were under attack for implementing radical change.

Some politicians turned against me, implied that I was too narrow-minded, and said I should take it easy on the black leadership. The conversation I had at the time with Congressman Charlie Rangel from Harlem was heated, as Rangel accused me of running my administration as if I wanted to be a one-term mayor. I told Charlie he was right, that's exactly what I was doing. But I told him that was why I would be a three-term mayor. I intuitively knew that creating, implementing, and sticking to the vision I had for the future to help those in poverty would provide me with several more terms as mayor.

Another way I was able to meet my goal during my first term was by using water to add to the city's coffers. That's right, water. Hundreds of institutions in the city owed a lot of money—hundreds of thousands of dollars—for their use of water that was provided by the city. But they never paid their water bills, until I came into office. Even the big universities— like Columbia and Fordham—owed money. I was not aware of this situation until a member of the Corporation Counsel's

Office—Edith Spivak, the oldest employee in that office—brought it to my attention. During her time there, Edith was involved in many of the most important issues facing the city, but I think this was one of her best moments.

Edith told me that the city sent out water bills and the foreign consulates, educational institutions, religious institutions, and charitable institutions all rejected the bills, never paying them, stating the bills were taxes to which they were not subject. She advised them, "No, they are service charges," and told them that their institution was subject to them. So she sent the bills with appropriate warnings of a cutoff of services. When the institutions still did not pay, she called some of them. One in particular was the Colombian mission to the United Nations. Edith told them that unless she received a certified check that afternoon for all unpaid back payments, she would personally come up and cut the water off. The Colombian mission paid. Most of the other institutions also paid when they learned of the consequences of not paying.

The religious institutions did an end run around us by going to the state legislature, which subsequently passed legislation providing some exemptions for smaller institutions. On the whole, however, we enjoyed a great success.

How Public Speaking Creates My Buzz

Giving speeches comprises a large part of sharing my vision, and it always has. All of my speeches are done extemporaneously. However, as off the cuff as I am in public speaking, I like to have a formal speech with me in case I blank out. Fortunately, I've never had to resort to reading a speech in this context. I usually take an hour to go over my notes, and those notes are constantly revised and upgraded. I *never* read my speeches and I advise anyone else not to do so either.

If part of creating your vision requires you to speak publicly and you are afraid of doing so, ask yourself, "Why?" Resolve that those reasons are not representative of who you are, and just practice, practice, practice. If you know your material, it shouldn't matter if there are five or five thousand people in the audience—you can be the expert.

My formula for creating buzz is based on the most important aspects of my presentation:

- Knowledge
- Integrity
- Personal authenticity
- Fearlessness
- Respect of myself and others
- Listening to others
- Letting others reply
- But. . . . .refuting them with the facts where appropriate

My vision for my role as a public speaker, as *New York Times* reporter Haberman was able to pick up on, is to make an impact and be relevant by stating facts. Plus, it's how I use my facial expressions with my words, which will show either my enthusiasm or my lack of interest in a way that words alone may not convey. Depending on the venue and purpose, it is always my intention to entertain and educate, and generally to do both.

I think one of the most important speeches I have ever given took place in Florida in 2004 before a group of Jewish Democratic senior citizens, when I sought to persuade them to vote for George W. Bush.

In the speech, I acknowledged the debt that all Americans

owed to FDR and the Democrats for saving the country from fascism during the Depression, and to FDR for his leadership in World War II. But I also pointed out how FDR failed the Jews by not using his enormous popularity to persuade Americans to overcome their then anti-Semitism and to open American doors to the German Jews who were permitted by Hitler to leave Germany.

I told them the story of the SS *St. Louis* carrying 937 passengers, all Jews who expected Cuba would accept them. After Cuba would not, all efforts to get special permission to land in Florida were rejected by FDR's administration, particularly the State Department. Most Jews and many historians believed the State Department was anti-Semitic, and FDR's defenders would say the country was as well. Therefore, any indication that FDR was helping the Jews would be counterproductive to our being able to help the English in their battle against the Nazis. The U.S. population was not willing to go to war to save the Jews from Hitler!

Those in the audience, while associating themselves with the New Deal and Roosevelt, nevertheless knew that my reference to the SS *St. Louis* was true. They knew that more than half of those people on board, after they had returned to Europe, ended up in concentration camps where they were murdered. During this speech, the key emotions I projected were poignancy, tenderness, and truthfulness.

Jews as a community have always overwhelmingly supported the Democratic Party simply because of the liberal political tradition that exists among Jewish voters. They are a mainstay of the Democratic Party. I wanted them to know that notwithstanding the importance of FDR's role during the Depression and during World War II, there was an enormous failure on the part of FDR. That failure was his unwillingness to save thousands of Jews who could have been saved had they been given entry into the United States. For that failure, I believe FDR resides not in heaven but in purgatory.

I was there to get votes for George W. Bush from the Jewish

community in Florida. I was successful as a result of that performance. The Bush campaign believes that I caused—by my comments in Florida and similar ones elsewhere—a substantial increase in the number of Jews voting for a Republican presidential candidate for the first time in their lives. I said at the time that I didn't agree with the president on a single domestic issue, but I believed his strong opposition to Islamic terrorism overrode domestic issues.

While most of my speeches have been successful—and I've made thousands—there have been times when I felt a speech failed to make the necessary impact. In the fall of 2005, I spoke before hundreds of people at an IBM convention: two speeches, on two consecutive days and to different audiences. The first day, I did not feel well and it showed in my remarks. Indeed, I found myself stumbling over words and was thinking, am I having a stroke? Which, thankfully, I was not. But I knew I wasn't connecting with the audience. They were not laughing at my anecdotes.

I told the IBM director that I would not charge for the presentation—$10,000. At first, he declined my offer, but after I persisted he accepted it. He also said he would be taking a poll of those in attendance, as he always did, on the quality of the speakers. There were about 100 people in the audience each day and he subsequently told me of the 200 people polled in the two audiences, only five did not rate me highly. So, apparently, I was better than I imagined. Nevertheless, I was not paid for the first day's speech. I asked the director to reconsider and allow me to withdraw my offer of non-payment and he declined, as was his right. No hard feelings on my part.

Each year I make about twelve to twenty speeches, and I have rarely turned down a paid engagement to speak if I could accommodate it on my schedule. When I was mayor, congressman, and city councilman, I never accepted fees or an honorarium for appearing before any group. I believed only the government could pay me during my time in public office. Now, however, I insist on being paid when speaking before local or national groups. When a group says in protest, "We are a charitable group and shouldn't have to pay for your services," I reply, "So are they all. But you do pay the caterer, and I am the entertainment, or the reason some people will attend." I make few exceptions.

How I Craft My Vision to Give a Great Speech

1. I tell the audience what I am currently doing.

2. I describe prominent political people I have met in my lifetime, such as:

- Presidents George Bush and George W. Bush
- President Ronald Reagan
- President Bill Clinton
- Anwar Sadat
- Menachim Begin
- Mayor David Dinkins
- Mayor Rudy Giuliani
- Mayor Michael Bloomberg
- Heads of State

3. I then discuss the issues of the day, such as the war of civilizations—international terrorism—facing us, the difference between Democratic and Republican philosophies, and those issues that change in interest from week to week, such as fair taxation, Social Security, China and trade, and the Kyoto Protocol.

4. I always encourage questions, if possible for a half-hour but at least for fifteen minutes. I love questions, and I'm good at answering them. You should always allow a follow-up question, if time permits, but not get into a debate.

5. I end my presentations with anecdotes that will typically generate a lot of laughter from the audience. Since I never tell jokes, I share only real-life anecdotes recalling incidents I have personally lived through. People love truthful tales, as you'll read below.

Mother Teresa and the Chocolate Chip Cookies

After my stroke in 1987, the doctors prescribed a week of rest for me at Gracie Mansion. I had been hospitalized for four days at Columbia Presbyterian Hospital. At the end of the week, on a hot Sunday afternoon in August, I was sitting on the porch. The police guard calls me on the phone and says, "Mr. Mayor, a car drove up with four nuns, and one of them says she's Mother Teresa. She would like to see you." I replied, "I know Mother Teresa. It is hardly possible she is down at the gate, but I'll come right down." I went down, and it indeed was Mother Teresa. I said, "Mother, what are you doing here?" She said, "Ed, I heard you were ill, you are in my prayers, and I came to see you." I replied, "Mother, your prayers have worked, and I'm recovered, but now that you are here, stay a while with me."

She and the three sisters got out of the car. I took her by the hand and she and I skipped up the walk to the porch. Behind us were the three sisters also skipping up the walk, and it all looked just like a movie. We chatted on the porch, and I said, "Mother, everybody believes you are a saint for all the good work you do, and I would like to do something for you. Is there anything I can do for you?" She replied, after thinking a moment, "Yes." I asked, "What, Mother?" She said, "I need two parking places in front of my AIDS hospice in the Village." I replied, "You have them." After all, even a saint has to park.

Then my chef, Mitchel London, came out onto the porch with freshly made lemonade and chocolate chip cookies. I poured the lemonade for all of us. I drank it; they did not. I said, "Mother, why aren't you drinking the lemonade?" She replied, "Ed, my sisters and I work primarily in India, where if a family were to offer to us what you are offering, it would cost them a week's wages. So, when we go into the home of a wealthy person or a poor person, we always decline food and drink. Everyone knows this, so the poor are not insulted." What a marvelous concept, I thought. She is definitely a saint.

I then said to her, pointing to the chocolate chip cookies, "Mother, these chocolate chip cookies are the best cookies ever made." She replied, "Good, wrap them up!"—meaning of course that she would take them with her and not be breaking her rule. The story always gets great laughter.

One Vote I Lost

Here's another story I often share with my audiences that always gets a laugh. When December 31, 1989 came and went, my twelve years as mayor living at Gracie Mansion also ceased. Several friends packed the refrigerator at my new home on lower Fifth Avenue. At the end of the following week, the refrigerator was empty and I decided to go shopping for the first time in twelve years. I went downstairs in the late morning intending to go to Balducci's, a market at 6th Avenue and 9th Street.

As I walked up Fifth Avenue and across 9th Street, about ten people on the street or on their stoops said to me, "Nice to have you back, Mayor," or, "You were a good mayor," or, some other positive comment. When I got to Balducci's, there in front of the door was a young man, about 30, standing with his bicycle. He looked at me and said, "You were a terrible mayor." I looked back and instantly responded, "Fuck you." I immediately felt liberated. He got on his bike without another word and rode off.

I have told this story to mixed-gender audiences, to audiences comprised largely of women or largely of men and on at least one occasion, an audience with several nuns, and on every occasion, without exception, everybody roared with laughter.

My Version of Strategic Planning

It is my understanding that business leaders refer to crafting your vision in their terminology, calling it "strategic planning." Whatever the buzzword is today, when I was in office I simply articulated and described how I saw the present condition, and the desired future. None of what I would convey to the public was wishful thinking—all my communications have been based on my ideal state of how the mayor's office should be run or how a project should be organized and completed.

I didn't always have the amount of time I wanted to spend on strategic planning as mayor because of the problems the city was facing. For the bankruptcy problems I encountered when I first entered office, I didn't think of what I was doing as "strategic planning." I just wanted to save the city, so I cut expenses and found better managers to help use funds better, so the people of New York and I could sleep at night. I had no fear—there was no room for it. Some of my staff lamented my presentation as a bit threatening and caustic, but it had to be done.

Overall, creating a vision involves marrying your beliefs and creativity with specific goals. Some questions you can ask yourself include:

> **1.** What can you see happening several years from now? This is known as creating the vision.

2. What exactly are you targeting? These are your goals and objectives.

3. Who are you and what do you or your business stand for? The answer to this will help you define your mission statement.

Creating the Vision

Every leader has the capacity to be visionary. A true visionary is someone who recognizes a need or opportunity and, regardless of conventional wisdom and skeptics, does something about it. Vision isn't forecasting the future, it is creating the future by taking action in the present to prepare for it.

The ability to accommodate a vivid, imaginative conception of what you want to see happen can be powerfully motivating. Communicating in ways that instinctively appeal to people is an important part of turning your aim into reality. Put simply, a vision is "an image of your desired future," and it is always described in the present tense.

When I was discharged *from the Army in 1946, I decided to go to law school. My vision was that lawyers with trained minds can do anything and everything. I was right. I didn't know at the time what I really wanted to do, but I thought law school sharpens your mind and prepares you to do anything in the business world. I now think I really wanted to be an educator. Writing my Commentaries today has allowed me to become an educator.*

Keep in mind that creating a vision of your desired future can be met with great resistance, especially in the political arena. But no matter the resistance, I never allowed it to restrict my creativity or get in my way of achieving the vision I had in mind. That's not to say I've been inflexible, but you don't go into creating a vision with the notion of being immediately pliable. I don't mind walking alone if it means I am retaining my authenticity, particularly in reference to what I believe in.

Visioning is not some artsy concept, at least not for me. It is basically how to get from here to there. The "there" may well be many years off. That would be strategic thinking. The "there" might also be relatively close, and that would be tactical thinking. If you are always focused on the task in front of you, you may miss a glorious opportunity to achieve better results by not looking at the bigger picture.

My vision can be perceived as demanding excellence from myself and others. I am an ordinary man, but I am a hard worker with boundless energy. I don't think I was looking to tap into my leadership skills when I started participating in Greenwich Village politics in 1956, but two key lessons I have learned along the way are:

1. Create a vision and stay with it.

2. Don't take no for an answer.

Crafting your vision requires you to draw on your beliefs and your mission. You'll assess the concept of what it is you're trying to do, figure out ways to implement it based on your beliefs, and get to the place of realizing it through your hard effort. Politicians do this all the time. The first question to ask yourself is, what is doable? The second question is, what else should I strive for?

Sometimes the process can be frustrating because you are carving out something new for yourself and your business. The

Craft your vision *by focusing on the future and describing your organization as it will be, as if that future version already exists.*

Try this exercise. Imagine it is five years from today and you've created your most desirable outcome based on the vision you have for yourself or your business. Now you should describe this future as if you could really see it.

best advice I can give you is "Be Not Afraid," as the Catholic hymn goes.

The positive aspects of creating a vision are that it takes you out of very limited thinking, provides a direction, and identifies your purpose. When I was in office, I hired the best and the brightest, whether they had supported me or not. I did not fear hiring people who I believed were smarter than I am. I knew many smart people could not actually accomplish their goals and execute their strategies whereas I had the talent to do so.

When leaders or employers map out an image of where they want the company or organization to go, it quite often produces an increase in efficiency and production. Employees and staffers are encouraged and receive a boost in their confidence when you take them into your confidence. I did that with the top people in my administration. One example from when I was mayor was adopting a balanced budget a year ahead of time. This was an idea proposed by a deputy mayor after he heard it mentioned by a reporter. It was an improbable task, although some would have said impossible, but I liked it and implemented it.

One of the best questions *to ask yourself when mapping out your vision is, "What are my goals?"*

Setting Goals and Objectives

Setting a goal allows you to be more specific about your vision. You simply decide where you want to go by determining a direction. How you can measure that goal is your objective, because you're breaking the goal down into tasks that are measurable and time-oriented.

Sometimes I did not always have the luxury of time on my side to set goals or perform the best methods for achieving those goals. Nonetheless, when I look back and measure my accomplishments, I think I've done quite well.

I did wonder why, early on in my first term as mayor, the vendors used by the city were so bad. When I asked I was told that good vendors would not sell to us because we didn't pay them on time. I called a meeting of our top ten agencies, which made 80 percent of the city's purchases, and asked how we could get better vendors to sell to us.

One commissioner said, "We are now decentralized, so we must recentralize and pay all bills from one agency." She volunteered to do that. Another person, the OMB director, said, "No, we should not centralize. Instead, I need to buy some computers to handle this." I said, "If you do, how long before we pay on time?" He replied, "Two years." I clapped my hands and said, "No, what I'm going to do is publish every month which commissioners pay on time and which do not, in rank order."

They were unhappy with that and said so. I replied, "Get

If you need a mission statement, here's
how yours should be structured:

- Short enough to be catchy.
- The focus should highlight one common purpose.
- The more specific to the organization the better—do not make it a generic statement.
- What you write should be transparent and straightforward.
- The more proactive verbs you use, the better. Also, skip the jargon.

ready, I'm giving you thirty days to shape up, and I will publish the names in sixty days," which I did. When one commissioner saw his name in the papers as number ten, the worst, he came rushing in to me and said, "It will never happen again, Mr. Mayor." "How can you be sure?" I asked. He replied, "Because I called in my comptroller and told him if I am ever again number ten, it's your ass." He was never at the bottom again.

Creating a Mission Statement

Many strategic business consultants say that creating a mission statement is a reflection of your purpose and function. Some people need to put this in writing for themselves and their employees.

My purpose and function as mayor was to reverse the city's declining fortune and make it once again the international capital of finance, commerce, communications, and culture. I personally have never created a mission statement, nor did we have one that hung in the mayor's offices similar to the mission statements posted in the hallways of companies and hotel lobbies. I preferred to inspire employees by talking to them individually and in audiences.

People trusted me. I believe motivating others is done simply by setting the example for integrity, courage, common sense, hard work, and dedication.

Overall, mission statements often motivate those people who are connected to the organization or campaign. Another maxim that I kept on my City Hall desk was, "If you say it can't be done, you are right, you can't do it."

Chapter Five

HOW TO ENGAGE THE MEDIA

The media and I have always had a symbiotic relationship. They needed me to provide a story for the next day's paper, and I needed them to get my message out to the public. Today, the reporters still call me, but now it is for my insight and opinions on stories they are generating.

You can engage the media one of two ways: proactively, where you contact them with your story idea, or reactively, when they call you to be a source to substantiate their ideas. Much of the news I created was proactive, and I did it through the press conferences. When I was mayor, I was not deluged with media calls because of the number of regular and add-on press conferences I had during the day. As mayor, I would hold as few as two but sometimes up to seven press conferences a day.

I always tried—and still try—to treat the media with respect. If reporters arrived late to a press conference and asked me to repeat what I had said earlier, I always accommodated them, which they appreciated. I thought of our question-and-answer sessions as jousting and usually fun. I hoped they enjoyed them as well.

I believed the three different media that I dealt with—television, radio, and print— should occasionally be treated separately by way of exclusive interviews. With respect to the print media, I broke it down further into the daily publications and weekly community newspapers. I treated the latter with equal respect, which they didn't expect and they always appreciated. My basic premise was that if I addressed the three major components equally, I would ultimately get my story out. And I did. I knew that the media was not there to give me free publicity, but I was there to give them a story. Creating my buzz was a by-product.

My twelve years in the mayor's office allowed me wonderful opportunities to develop and maintain a great relationship with all the media, which I still enjoy today. I had no complaints, with rare exception, with anybody in the news business, even when I was attacked. And I've been through challenging times when journalists would write stories about me that were horrific.

The most challenging time for me was during the corruption crisis. I truly was in agony day after day, even though I had no business dealings with the two public officials—Donald Manes and Stanley Friedman, who had committed the corruption—nor was I in any way personally involved in their corrupt activities. But I was fearful that their corruption would tar me, or they would lie and, in exchange for a plea bargain, falsely seek to implicate me.

As long as the reporter who was writing the story presented my side accurately, for me it was a balanced interview.

Some reporters are known to be outstanding in their integrity. Others not as much, but I will omit names.

HOW REPORTERS (USUALLY) THINK

Reporters are bombarded with information on a daily basis and are under enormous pressure to file stories on tight deadlines. They love getting information no one else has or that is extremely valuable to them, and they want to know how your information can benefit readers or viewers. You need to know exactly what a reporter wants if you want to create buzz about you.

Journalists typically want news that answers the following questions:

- Why will readers and viewers be interested?
- How timely is your information?
- Are you a credible resource?

If you can back up your information with relevant data, figures and numbers, your relationship with a reporter is on its way. Reporters love anecdotes and a quip to close their story. I am good at providing both.

Cultivating Media Relations

One of the best ways for me to engage the media very early in my career was to appear on Dr. Martin Abend's television show back in the late 1970s. This was free publicity for me, which is the best type of publicity around.

I would appear on Abend's show every Friday night on a weekly basis. Anyone who remembers watching this show can recall Abend's in-your-face, screaming style. I took the opposite route—I remained calm and studied-looking. People on the street would stop and ask me why I didn't respond with similar passion. I reminded them I was, in my own way, but if I screamed, responsible people would not hear what I was saying. I created my own buzz by setting myself apart from the on-air verbal fracas and made friends by doing so.

Appearing on that show gave me some of the best free publicity I could ever have while I was in office. It was by far one of the most effective marketing tools I had at my disposal, and whatever issue was currently being debated I had the opportunity to give my opinion and spotlight for the public the issues important to me.

How I typically engage the media is by providing anecdotes as well as factual information. Every reporter is looking for a good story, and political stories, business stories—whatever they may be—are human interest stories, when it comes down to it. I believe the best asset you can have is a sense of humor, and I think I have that. Plus, I always try to speak in a conversational tone—that's who I am—and that is the best way to get your message across.

Candor is prized by the media and the public, and, as I said, an appropriate sense of humor is always helpful. Both are rare qualities—and should be cultivated.

When I was invited to a *New York Magazine* boardroom luncheon in the spring of 1979, the editors wanted to talk to me about the way I handle things. As I wrote in my book, *Mayor*, these editors felt I was not cautious enough, I was too available, and perhaps too candid. That made no sense to me, considering the alternatives.

I told them that even though I was not a congressman anymore and was now mayor, the power of the office I held had nothing to do with me and my personality. I was and always will be an honest ordinary guy with some special abilities. Sure, I am more direct than most public officials, and I love the opportunities that allow me to be that way.

There was a time that an interview injured me. In 1982 I was interviewed by a *Playboy* reporter, at his request. During the interview, which was conducted over a period of time totaling fifteen hours, I lost my perspective. For practiced politicians, there is a phenomenon of having a "governor" (a machine) in your head protecting you from making stupid statements, similar to a governor in a car that limits your speed. That protection lasts for about a half-hour—never fifteen hours.

The interviewer asked me about crime and dirt in the city, to which I replied, "Sure. Have you ever lived in the suburbs? I haven't, but I've talked to people who have, and it's sterile. It's nothing. It's wasting your life, and people do not wish to waste their lives once they've seen New York!"

The interviewer then asked why people would live in the city, given "lousy city services, late subways." I replied, "as opposed to wasting time in a car? Or, out in the country, wasting time in a pickup truck? When you have to drive 20 miles to buy a gingham dress or a Sears Roebuck suit? This rural America thing, I'm telling you, it's a joke."

I thought it was a very funny answer, but ultimately it was devastating for me. The article was published six months later, a few days after I had announced that I was running for governor of New York. According to many observers who followed that election, those comments more than anything else caused my defeat by Mario Cuomo.

I came to a different conclusion though. I think the upstate people decided that while they liked me personally, I was too devoted to the city and would not be fair to them in the distribution of government funding. I would have been very fair, but understandably they thought otherwise, and my hubris didn't help.

Aside from candor, integrity is the essential part of your body and mind in any field of endeavor. I know that is the core of my being. I never tell people something I don't believe with respect to my philosophy or an action I will be taking. One does not have to, on every matter and occasion, make a statement that you know will antagonize. You can defer responding by saying, "I'll think about it." But you should not lie. This has always stood me in good stead.

Integrity was essential in communicating my message. I never compromised that even if it meant forgoing income or an opportunity to be sought after by the media. The respect I gained from the public by following my standards meant that I worked with some of the best people in the media business, and those dealing with me accept my word. It is a great position to be in.

Getting Your Message Out

Be creative with the media in order to create buzz so you can stand out from the competition. Get people to notice you by being smart and confident—that is so important.

There are strategies you can use to build a great relationship with the media so that reporters always know they can count on you to fill space in their newspapers or on radio or television. Your goal should be to establish and develop and continually maintain your relationship with the media so they end up working for the vision you are creating for yourself. But you do need to do the legwork by knowing how, where, and when to pitch your story, and by having a good story to tell.

I knew how because I knew the issues firsthand, and I was able to address them with hungry reporters at my press conferences. And I did it consistently and reaped the benefits of getting my news and information out to the public. I still remain a reliable source to the media, as well as a relevant and, most importantly, trustworthy figure to the public.

TIPS ON HOW TO BUILD YOUR RELATIONSHIP WITH THE MEDIA

- Identify which reporters cover the subject in which you are an expert. Call or send a brief introductory letter inviting them to a breakfast or lunch to tell them who you are.
- Always be straightforward and honest with them. If you find yourself being asked questions to which you do not have answers, tell them you don't know but that you'll find out and get back to them.
- Respect their deadlines and meet them. If you do that, you will help build the relationship so they will consider you not just a credible resource but a dependable one.
- Do not lose your cool when responding to a reporter, as anything you say is on the record, no matter their assurance to the contrary. A newsworthy statement off the record will find its way to the public. You should endeavor to control the interview by staying focused and concise.
- Use the reporter's first name—I always do. It makes the interview friendlier, even while discussing the most hostile issues. Plus, it humanizes the conversation.
- Think of three key points you want to get across before any interview, and write them down on a memo pad. This way, when it comes time for the interview, you'll be more natural. How I got to be a good speaker was practice, practice, practice.
- If you do not appear in the story, do not be discouraged. It will happen.
- Be yourself.

I believe that one of the reasons my relationship with the media has always been good is because I generally know as much about the subject they are discussing with me as they do, if not more, and therefore I am not afraid of them as are many public officials. When public officials have this fear of reporters, it's because they have failed to educate themselves enough on the issues before they hold press conferences or are interviewed. By understanding the issues and studying the facts, I retain my confidence and am able to hold my own.

The best way to build and maintain an ongoing relationship with the media is to know what you're talking about—and if you don't, then educate yourself. Read books and articles on the subject, perform Internet research, interview experts who have blazed the trail before you—whatever it takes. Politicians or business leaders may have the passion to discuss their issue or market their product, but if it is not backed by knowledge, they are seen as nothing more than people who lack substance, or empty suits.

If a reporter calls you, *ask him or her for a description of the story and the deadline first before answering their questions. This way, if you need time to research something, you can do so and tell them you'll get back to them as soon as possible. Also, ask them to read your quotes back to you to ensure accuracy. I began the practice, followed by many today, to tape the interview—in effect, two dueling tape recorders.*

I have found that business people are generally not equipped to take on the media and build a persona without professional help. I believe that they are best served by retaining profession-als to assist them, at least until they become accustomed to deal-ing with the press. Having an intermediary will make it much easier and bring results earlier.

When I was preparing to run for mayor in 1973, at the sug-gestion of one of my staff, I took voice coaching classes as a way to be more presentation-friendly. I thought that was okay and a good idea because of my New York accent. My voice is distinctive, but too high-pitched, and while my vocabulary is excellent, my diction is not the best. So I went to a voice teacher for private lessons in speaking. I did very well in the voice exer-cises.

One day, I said to the instructor, "I hope you know that my coming here should be kept confidential." She said, "Of course." Then she said, "I have lots of clients who want their taking lessons to be confidential." Then to my horror, she rat-tled off the names of about ten of her clients, all well known in the media, government, or running for office like me. That was the last time I saw her.

Staying Relevant

Today I rely on my in-house news-clipping service that I created, and which my assistants help me with. I photocopy any newspa-per article referring to me or to the letters I write, and have copies sent out to good friends and some members of the media. It helps to keep me relevant, and it provides reporters with the latest information on what it is I am involved with, so that if they need a quote for a story, odds are some will remember and call me.

I currently do not have a website, but I will ultimately have one. It is a tool that absolutely allows members of the media to

MEDIA TOOLS YOU CAN USE

1. *The Press Release.* A written news release is the most accepted method for engaging the media. It gives details about your issue or event and provides the who, what, where, why, and when. When I was mayor, I had a press secretary and four or more people working under him or her, who would generate all our press releases.

Today, my weekly Commentaries are a form of a press release in that I send them out to all the media as a way of keeping them informed about my opinions regarding today's issues. For your own press releases, always include a contact phone number for a contact person, as well as the address of the event and the date and time.

2. *Database.* Comprehensive media database lists exist to help people get the word out about their campaigns and businesses. The least expensive route to finding these is at your local library, where they are free. These databases typically categorize reporters by media and geographical area. Some are divided by topic and cultural entities.

3. *E-mail.* Should you call reporters or e-mail them? It sounds simple, but e-mail is a better way to communicate with reporters. Most newspapers, television stations, and magazines have websites with contact information for editors and reporters. In this age of computers and digital cameras, most reporters would prefer to receive a news release pitch with a photo by e-mail. If you have questions, call and ask an assistant editor. But don't waste their time pitching the story over the phone. Assignment editors worth their salt will ask for written documentation of your story, event, news conference, etc.

They will either give you a fax number or an e-mail address for submitting your information.

stay on top of what it is you're doing, so you may engage them in the buzz you're working on.

At the moment, all of my material appears on the website of the La Guardia and Wagner Archives of LaGuardia Community College, which has catalogued all of my past and current material.

I think the Internet is an incredible gift to those who write and would like their writings read. I am one of them. A member of the gym I belong to, whom I do not know, once said, "Mayor, I understand you are a blogger [technically not true, since I do not have a website]. Could I get copies of your Commentaries?" I felt very good that he independently asked to be put on my e-mail list. Whenever an opportunity presents itself to obtain e-mail addresses from acquaintances and audiences that I address, I take advantage of it and add them to my list. If you would like to receive my Commentaries, you may contact me directly at eikoch@bryancave.com.

Today, anyone who is interested in pressing their views to the point of putting out what is almost a magazine with unlimited circulation at a nominal cost, can do so. I do believe that there are many people in this country who are now receiving my Commentaries by e-mail, either directly or forwarded by others, and reading them in website magazines (such as NewsMax, for which I write a column for their website and their print magazine). These people are now aware of me who otherwise would not be.

As I said, my relationship with the media has always been good. Joe Klein, columnist for *Time* magazine and author of several books on politics, used a quote from me in one of his books, something like "Pick a dozen issues. If you agree with me on eight out of twelve, you should vote for me. If you agree with me on twelve out of twelve, see a psychiatrist." Klein told me in the fall of 2006 he thought two of the best politicians he's ever seen at work are Mario Cuomo and me.

Ken Auletta, a columnist for the *New Yorker,* spoke about

me and my thirty-plus-year relationship with the media in a panel group discussion in October 2005. He said, "[Mayor Koch] spoke his words sharply, and the press loved hearing that. And he had this way of standing up to people and not trying to placate them."

That was and still is true.

Chapter Six

ATTRACTING LOYAL FOLLOWERS

To create loyal followers, there are two rules I live by: First, be a good follower. Second, be a good leader. From there, you will develop great relationships with loyal supporters.

While maintaining my independence and ability to criticize, I also support and champion others. Most of us begin our careers this way.

I did not begin my political career as a leader. I was a lawyer and then a street speaker. I find it to be rare that anyone immediately steps into a leadership position. That is why learning how to be a good follower comes first. I do not believe that there are good leaders who are not good followers. We all are followers at one time or another. If everyone tried to be a leader at the same time, nothing would ever get accomplished.

If you don't like the word "follower," pick another word that suits you—perhaps "supporter." When I was mayor, what I needed the most—and received—was support to accomplish my goals.

Even if your goal is to be a leader and you find yourself in a follower role at this time, how you approach your job or position today may determine your ultimate success or failure as a leader. Sometimes you may not like being a follower, but if you stick with your vision and your plan, as I discussed in Chapter 4, you will end up being a leader at some point.

Until then, you may encounter times when you may not feel like you want to do what you need to do. My advice is to do it anyway, because the price you pay for not following through on tasks could be serious and diffuse any solid buzz you could be creating for yourself along the way. It is better for people to say you are a good worker and will become a great leader, than to have the buzz about you say that you are uncooperative and lazy—and will never become a leader who is effective or admired. Followership is essential for progress.

Motivation is crucial to being a good follower. Here are a few rules of thumb that help me and may help you stay motivated:

- First, establish a schedule and stick to it.
- Second, communication is a two-way street. I like people and like to share my experiences, doubts, successes, and failures with friends. Most important, I am also a good listener. My advice: Let others talk and feel involved with you.
- Third, life is not always sweet and easy. Be prepared to do your share of the heavy work, unpleasant as it may be. If it is not worth doing or is not providing you some satisfaction, get out of what you are seeking and find some other goal.

The equation for success for a follower is very similar to that for a leader. The more of these traits (tools) you have successfully developed, the greater the probability of your success, either as a follower or as a leader. Following leads to a position of leadership.

Each day will not be easy. *Always think you are being tested. It is the thought of achieving my goals that keeps me motivated.*

Focus on the goals to be achieved. Having a goal to work toward can be very motivating and rewarding. For every goal you set, you may be working with others, and there will be the workers and the drones. Be a worker. Never be a drone. It will haunt you as people remember you as a shirker, someone who let other people do the work.

I am loyal and people can count on me. That is why I have been successful. People love to support me because of these characteristics. Remember, people will forgive differences of opinion, if they believe in your sincerity.

As a follower (and ultimately as a leader trying to attract loyal followers), regardless of your job, you do have responsibilities. What makes a good follower? Telling the truth. Honesty— along with dependability—rank high on the priority list for both followers and leaders.

Never follow an unethical person. *If you detect the person designated as leader is dishonest or unethical, get off the train.*

Other significant characteristics that define a good follower include:

• *What type of individual you are.* I have never thought of myself as being charismatic, yet people think I am. Why? I believe it is attributed to my candor, integrity, and willingness to stay with issues I believe in, no matter how unpopular.

• *How well you communicate with others.* Learn to speak in easy-to-understand, direct language. Do not be afraid to voice disagreement, but always do so courteously without patronizing.

• *How well prepared you are.* If you are able to cull as much information as possible about your or your group's goals, you will be able to be more organized and grow into a leadership role.

• *How cognizant you are of other people and what they desire, what they need, and the goals they trying to attain.* I am candid, but I am sensitive to other people's wants and needs. Both as a follower and a leader, I have had a genuine interest in other people, which has fostered trust by others. As mayor, that may have come with the job because of the issues I supported. But it was my ability to listen that helped me be a good follower *and* a good leader.

• *How well you evaluate your options.* That means being patient and persistent and using sound judgment to discern what is most important, depending on your particular situation. Don't hesitate to correct mistakes and admit error.

• *How consistently you recognize contributions by others.* Many employers subscribe to the notion that if you are doing a good job, they won't tell you, but if you are not, they will. I do not agree with that. Whenever possible, always give credit, especially if someone has worked hard. People like to be rewarded, even if the reward is only a compliment.

Even if you do not have all of these characteristics, they can be developed over time. Here are some questions that leadership coaches suggest asking yourself so that you may develop your followership—and ultimately leadership—skills:

- How cooperative am I in working with others to achieve a goal? The idea here is to be helpful and supportive while pursuing a mutually beneficial goal.
- How loyal, dedicated, and dependable am I to the group's endeavors? Being loyal and faithful to the group's endeavors hones skills of trustworthiness and dedication.
- Am I able to be honest and practical by sharing positive feedback? Constructive criticism can be beneficial to help steer the group toward its goal.
- How receptive am I to other people's ideas? This means being alert, sensitive, and respectful of what other people are thinking—a required skill for being a good leader.

Being a Good Leader Creates Loyal Followers

I believe that being a great leader requires you to accept the fact that you are influencing situations or events to change, and you do so by motivating and managing your business or your political campaign in such a way so as to implement those changes.

I also believe leadership is in the genes, and that leaders can also be created by hard work and dedication. Charisma may be in the DNA, but hard work, decency, and accomplishment can create charisma. I think I have the genes but believe I am overwhelmingly in the second category. Leadership normally requires charisma, which is an aura that is a gift from God or the result of a lot of hard work and dedication to a goal.

How I Did It

I have been an activist all my life. Often I was simply among the crowd, sometimes I worked with the top organizers, and occasionally I became the leader of the group. What's important is doing the job right, exhibiting your special abilities and talents, and distinguishing yourself. Good leaders recognize the successful efforts of others.

When I helped organize citizens in Greenwich Village to support the candidacy of Adlai Stevenson for president, I started by volunteering to speak for him on the street. I was a lawyer at the time, and I had no experience speaking on street corners. Standing on a box addressing passersby was unnerving, but I did it. As in most cases, doing something regularly results in increased confidence. It wasn't long before I was considered to be the best among the half-dozen people speaking on the street in Greenwich Village for Stevenson.

I learned the keys to success, which were obvious to me at the time and are principles I still agree with: *Know your subject and the issues*. I did that by devouring the newspapers every morning. And I deliberately argued with people about election issues, which honed my debating skills. Those arguments allowed me to test my logic before mounting the box on a street corner.

I found the process to be similar when I ran for office. I supported dozens of candidates before running for office myself. Having supported other candidates taught me to be a better candidate. It also brought to the campaign the loyalty of others who had seen me work for candidates by addressing envelopes, making telephone calls, and ultimately becoming the top speaker for Stevenson in Greenwich Village, a tough environment.

As with so many endeavors, *practice, practice, practice* is the way to get to the top. Losing in 1962 made me realize how little I knew about government. As a result, I studied and became an expert.

Holding public office was not just a job for me—it was a calling. I believe that God put me on this earth providing me with opportunities to improve the lives of my fellow citizens, and I honestly believe that I fulfilled my obligations in that respect.

Why Trust Is the Hallmark of a Great Leader

What allows people to trust you? It is obvious—your perceived honesty. Honesty and integrity are synonymous. I'm talking about both fiscal and intellectual integrity. Some of one, but not the other, is not enough. A little bit of both is not enough either. You need both to the fullest to be a leader. And I am not talking only about perception, because some people may be initially perceived as honest, but are later uncovered as something less than that. You must be totally trustworthy to be and remain a great leader.

Some examples of people who were born great leaders are Franklin Delano Roosevelt, Jack Kennedy, Robert Kennedy, and Fiorello LaGuardia. A great leader who was created by circumstances was Harry Truman. He rose to the occasion.

As I have said, I do not believe that I have charismatic qualities. I am not an intellectual. I am not an athlete. I believe people believe in me because they trust me. They know that I will never betray them. They also like my candor, spirit, and good humor. Yes, I am being repetitious, but I want to hammer home the message.

As people see someone successfully rise, they begin to see other characteristics they never saw before. They see you as a presence. Not necessarily handsome or strong or physically appealing, but as a presence. Suddenly they see you and your success as special. You dominate the room you enter as soon as you enter it. Former President Bill Clinton becomes the center of attention of every room he enters.

One of the prime examples of another current political leader who does this would be Hillary Clinton. Other obvious leaders today include John McCain, Barack Obama, and Rudy Giuliani. Along with Hillary Clinton, as of this writing, they are all running for president. People admire their success, and each has a certain mystery to their persona.

In addition to presence, other important characteristics of a great leader are integrity, accountability, vision, passion, innovation, and trustworthiness. The American Management Association asked a panel of academics and experts some years ago what the most essential skills were for effective leadership. At the top of the list was integrity. I completely agree. A person with integrity is seen as honorable, and without anything else will be admired.

What I Accomplished Using These Techniques

After being elected mayor, I occasionally felt unqualified to respond to various crises. Then I would remind myself that the public had many capable candidates to vote for when they voted for mayor, such as Mario Cuomo, Abe Beame, Bella Abzug, and Herman Badillo, yet they chose me. And although there are undoubtedly lots of people who could do a better job than I could, they chose not to run for office. So all I could do was the best job I was capable of doing, which is what I did.

During my mayoralty, I had to do many things that had an adverse impact on the poor living in New York City, who were dependent on city services. The middle class and rich can move, as some did. And they can also use their own money to pay for services—such as education, sanitation, police, and parks—which deteriorate when the city is on the edge of bankruptcy. The poor are not able to do that and suffer the most.

A LIST OF MY LOYAL FOLLOWERS

Everyone has friends who have helped them. I'll list a few of mine who have been with me for many years:

John LoCicero's political career has been tied to mine since I met him in the early 1960s. He served in my mayoralty as a special assistant, which meant he was there when I needed him and got things done. He was a supporter and colleague going back to the early days of my political career.

Pete Piscitelli was my emissary to Albany. His knowledge and integrity made it possible for me to get things done up there. I met him when I became mayor and was choosing the people who would help me run the government. We remain friends today.

Bruce and Mary Barron are special friends, not in government but always as confidants and providing advice on the delivery of health care. Bruce and Mary were close friends of Dan Wolf, who was the editor of the *Village Voice* and is now deceased. Dan Wolf was the wisest man I ever knew.

Jim Gill, my law partner, and I for years have had lunch two or three times a week and have never come away bored with one another.

Henry Stern is another loyal follower. Our friendship goes back nearly fifty years.

Other friends include:

George Arzt, one of my mayoral press secretaries.
Peter Aschkenasy, a campaign treasurer in several campaigns.
Arnie Kriss, an active political campaigner.

And two women, Ronay Menschel and Diane Coffey, who served in both my congressional and mayoral offices, and with whom I maintain wonderful relationships.

While I do not regret reducing services—which was necessary to balance the budget and resurrect the city—I do regret that I caused pain to people and didn't adequately explain why it was happening. Today the city has surpluses in the billions of dollars because of what we did during the twelve years of my administration and the good works of the mayors who followed.

Probably the one incident more people recall from my mayoralty would be the subway strike of 1980. People thought the city would be crippled, as it was during the subway strike under Mayor John Lindsay in 1966. No, under me, the people of the City of New York decided we would stand up to the city employees in the Transit Workers' Union, who were engaged in an illegal strike. Municipal workers are not allowed by law to strike. Instead, we have binding arbitration for most unions when an impasse is reached.

I kept the city alive and functioning by encouraging people to walk across the five bridges that connect Manhattan to the other boroughs. I had a confrontation with a union supporter on the Brooklyn Bridge who said to me as I exhorted people to walk over the bridge, "You are nothing but a strike-breaker." I replied, "And you're nothing but a wacko."

My reply, including the word "wacko," became part of a banner headline the next day in newspapers reporting the incident. My advice: A leader should be out front leading. People will remember. A major error President George Bush made was to fly over New Orleans during Hurricane Katrina rather than walk the streets in hip boots.

I have now been out of office for seventeen years, and I think it is fair to say that people recall my mayoralty with a sense of appreciation for the job I did. They smile and say nice things when they stop me on the street to chat.

I have been given opportunities, no doubt. Interestingly, many public officials are reluctant to admit they believe in God. I do believe in God and call on God all the time to help me, and

I am not religious. But I know there was something before the Big Bang. I know that creation—the world with all of its complexity—could not have happened by itself. I believe in evolution, but I also believe in the hand of God. This all didn't just happen by chance. I say all of this on appropriate occasions and it has helped me. It has given me confidence and the confidence of others.

I am grateful for my successes. They helped me develop a loyal following—people who trusted in me and my judgment—that continues to this day. While many public officials go into oblivion when they leave office, I have not. People recall the major successes of my twelve years. Four of these successes include:

1. *Balancing the Budget.* This hadn't been done in at least fifteen years. The budget had become hugely unbalanced over the years, beginning with at least the last two years of Mayor Bob Wagner's administration, followed by Mayors Lindsay and Beame spending money for services that the city did not have. Under them, the city borrowed money to pay operating bills.

2. *Returning a Sense of Pride to New Yorkers.* Leadership, candor, and humor allowed me to give back to the people of New York City their pride. When the city was on the edge of bankruptcy, New Yorkers sometimes introduced themselves saying, "I'm from Long Island." During my administration they were proud to say once again, "I'm from New York City." This pride continues today.

3. *Building Affordable Housing.* As mayor, I am very proud of having created approximately 250,000 rent-affordable housing units with city dollars.

4. *Changing the Judicial Selection System.* I changed the judicial selection system in New York City, where the mayor appoints criminal and family court judges. I appointed 140 such judges during my twelve-year mayoralty, eliminating all political involvement. That system is still in effect under Mayor Michael Bloomberg.

Why I Was Successful

One thing that made my role as a leader successful: I was visible. I am by nature a shy person, but I stretched myself to become a public person. This requires constant practice and doing, which ultimately becomes easier.

I have spoken before crowds as often as possible without, I hope, seeming foolish. I knew, and still do know, when not to speak. For example, I introduced Simon and Garfunkel to 500,000 people on the Great Lawn of Central Park. Normally, a mayor would have gone into a long spiel welcoming the crowd. I did not, knowing that under such circumstances, the crowd would be angry at anyone delaying the entertainment with a speech. So I merely said, without mentioning my name (I knew they knew who I was), "Ladies and gentlemen, Simon and Garfunkel." They even kept my introduction on the commercial record released of the concert.

And, finally, if you want to create loyal followers, as I did:

- Be accurate in what you say. Do not exaggerate or offer an opinion when you do not really have a thoughtful answer. Wait for the moment when you do have a substantive and meaningful comment.
- Try not to create unnecessary enemies, but also know that you are best known and respected because of the enemies you make. So it's a question of common sense and balance.
- Above all, be not afraid.

Part Three

TRUSTING YOUR PLAN

Incredible talent exists in this great country of ours to confront national issues, such as the elimination of homelessness, drug abuse, racism, violence, and crime. Unfortunately, this talent is not used sufficiently because the issue that receives the most attention from a candidate or incumbent is what they believe will assure election or reelection.

During my political career, I was more concerned about serving the people well than getting reelected. It sounds grandiose, but I knew I could always make a living if I lost an election. Yes, in order to serve the people I spent countless hours campaigning to get reelected, but my primary goal was to serve the people of New York City well. I was not dominated by thoughts of power, control, or riches. I am sure this self-evaluation will be viewed by some readers as sophomoric on my part. Ultimately in 1989, when I ran for a fourth term, the voters did throw me out. Most would concur that when they got Mayor David Dinkins in my place, they did not get a better mayor. Here I am seventeen years later still working and enjoying myself. But I will confess there is no better job than mayor of New York City.

I am not saying that none of our elected representatives are similarly motivated. But that attitude is not the coin of the realm.

My goal here is to educate you on how to tap into your talents and stay with the common sense principles of personal ethics—integrity, honesty, self-worth, compassion, and, yes, the desire to do good—so that you trust yourself. If you trust yourself, then most of your decisions will be the right ones, and buzz will begin to happen because people will trust you.

So, how do you get people to listen to you? Vote for you? Support you? Follow you? Buy your product? The answer to those questions is whether *you* would want to listen to you, vote for you, support you, follow you, or buy your own product.

If you don't trust yourself, then your plan cannot succeed. It is corny to say it, but say it I will. I am just an ordinary guy with some special talents and faith in God. It all works for me.

Chapter Seven

WHY YOUR GUT RULES EVERY TIME

When it comes to weighing choices, I have found that my gut response is generally an educated one, because it is based on my experiences of everyday life. Remember, as of this writing, I am 82 years old. That's a lot of experience.

I operated my mayoral office by relying on experts in particular fields. In most cases, those experts were the commissioners I appointed. When an issue arose, I would ask the commissioners to come to my office and bring two or three of their best staff people with them.

Present at most meetings would be my executive administrator Ronay Menschel, chief of staff Diane Coffey, and corporation counsel Allen Schwartz. The agency commissioner involved would attend with several of their staff people. During our meetings, I would ask the commissioner and each staff person their opinion, no matter what position they held. At the end of the presentations, I would ask questions to be sure I understood as much as possible about the issue.

Generally, relying on the intelligence of experts helped me formulate a decision. But that is only half the equation. The other half required using my instincts to decide which option would be the best one. When I thought I sufficiently understood the matter and felt ready to make a decision, I would clap my hands and say, "Okay, now this is what we are going to do," and I would outline in detail how we were going to move forward.

Much research has been reported on how people sometimes use their intuition without the use of a rational process, because they have a "sixth sense." When I was the mayor of New York City, I chose to use more educated information *and* my intuition in my decision-making process. This is who I am and what I believe. Responsible people should rely on their intellect and life experience in reacting to situations. Incorporated in the experience of that situation is your gut reaction and intuition.

Decision-making is a melding of both rationality and intuition. In advance of publishing a Commentary, I always send it to four of my friends and ask for their opinion or criticism. Many times they will suggest changes, which I accept and then insert in my own language, or sometimes I reject the suggestions. Advice and criticism from others is very important.

How I Used My Instincts While in Office

When I was a congressman, I had a staff of ten people during my first term. I hired five people to work in my New York City office and five for my Washington, D.C. office. I had been elected by a margin of victory provided by the Liberal Party, which had given me its election line by endorsing me, the Democratic Party candidate.

The Democratic Party made no demands on me to hire any of their people to work in my office. I chose my staff regardless of party affiliation by selecting those who I hoped were the best and the brightest.

However, I did receive a call from a high-ranking member of the Liberal Party, saying they were very upset that I had not selected anyone from their party to work on my staff. It was made clear to me that not doing so endangered my relationship with the Liberal Party in the future. Their demand was not unreasonable. Indeed, it was what was expected after nearly every election, especially in a case like mine where their line carried the day for me. They took the position that they had elected me and getting a job for one out of ten people hired was not an onerous demand on their part.

I said okay and hired a person presented to me by the Liberal Party to be my secretary. I was sorry to make an exception to my rule of no patronage hiring, but I am not suicidal. Regrettably, in my judgment the secretary's skills were not adequate to the job. I called the Liberal Party official and said, "I simply cannot go on this way. How do I get rid of her?" He said, "Find her another job."

A member of my staff called Bill Green, regional head of HUD, and explained our need to find a job for her. He said, "Send her over. I will be happy to help." Fortunately, she decided to find her own job and did. All's well that ends well.

How Trust Plays a Role

Trusting yourself and your instincts builds confidence. By trusting yourself, you will be able to make sound decisions and ultimately create the buzz you are seeking. Citing the example above, I was able to reaffirm for my future decisions to trust my gut—and not to participate in patronage hiring ever again on my staff.

Self-trust is at the core of knowing why your gut rules every time. When you are creating buzz about yourself, you must trust the message you tell yourself. If you don't believe your message and vacillate, your followers will not believe you either, and your campaign or business may falter.

When you have a structured *and disciplined plan you follow and something distracts you, your gut will tell you that sticking to your original plan is the right thing to do. Trust that feeling; don't allow yourself to get sidetracked.*

Here's another illustration of my technique that occurred when I was mayor. We had run out of jail cells. There was a danger that judges would order the city to release prisoners before we put more convicted offenders in jail. I was told by the Corrections Agency that we could not build any more cells on Rikers Island, New York City's largest jail facility, because of environmental concerns. And building somewhere other than Rikers would be nearly impossible. It is difficult to get permission to build prisons in communities, which generally resist such city services. They want jails, but they want them in someone else's neighborhood.

I said to the commissioner, "Bring your top ten people to my office every day [setting the hour] and we will discuss this matter for an hour a day no matter how long it takes until someone comes up with the solution." After four days, one person came up with the idea of how we could build several thousand more cells on the Island and stay within the environmental laws. The staff people attending those daily meetings were just plain tired of sitting in my office like children at school. My plan worked.

Discipline is extremely important in exercising your intuitive muscle. This is one of the characteristics that make certain CEOs very successful. They use their business logic or consult with other experts to help expand their gut feeling to make a decision. There also are examples of how intuition plays a role in decision making for some entrepreneurs. They take great risks because they know what to do instinctively, and they just go out and do it. However, my advice is to rely on your intellect and life experience in reacting to situations and use your gut instinct based on those prior experiences as your decision-making guide.

What if You Are Wrong?

The American public loves the person who makes a mistake and admits it publicly. You get more friends and supporters by admitting errors and advancing an amended proposal than by being considered infallible. No one likes someone, except in religious matters, who is never wrong. People want to forgive others for their errors. It makes them feel better.

I once fired a commissioner. She actually quit when I imposed ridiculous conditions on her performance as commissioner, and so in a most refined way, she resigned. I knew almost immediately that she was right and I was wrong. On one of my television programs, I admitted the error in my judgment. People—including the former commissioner—responded with kudos. But she never came back to work.

Obviously, I don't recommend making mistakes so that others can forgive you, but I do recommend risking a mistake in pursuit of excellence. Again, be not afraid.

How to Use Your Intuition

If after you have received input from your experts, carefully analyzed all your options, and weighed the choices against your own intellect and life's experiences, you are still unsure what decision to make, there are ways to stimulate your intuition to help you finalize your decision. This is especially applicable for those people who are embarking on a new career path, who may not have experience under their belt to tap into or do not yet have the luxury of expert resources available. Try simple contemplation to connect with the intuition muse.

An illustration of communing with the muse and coming up with a common sense solution is best demonstrated by the following anecdote. I made it a policy never to tell the police department, the police commissioner, or anyone else in authority how to handle a police matter. One weekend when I was out in Quogue, Long Island, I learned when turning on the news on Sunday morning that there had been a riot in the East Village. All of the radicals, squatters, and homeless people had decided to violate the regulation that enforced closing the city parks by 1 A.M. so the parks wouldn't be taken over by those who believed they owned them, and who used them in ways that mothers and children couldn't use them the next day because the parks were so filthy from the night before.

When I called the chief in charge and asked for a report, he said, "Mayor, they are coming back tonight but this time, we will be ready for them." I thought all we needed was another riot in August. But, I didn't want to order him to take a different course of action. So instead I said, "Chief, isn't the temperature hot and rising in the city?" He said, "Yes." I said, "Most of these people don't have air conditioning." He said, "Yes." I said, "Wouldn't it make sense to lift the curfew for Sunday night because of the weather, encouraging people to sleep in the park that night?" He said, "Yes." And then he added, "Mayor, that is a very good idea." I have no doubt he wanted to avoid a second riot as much as I did. On Monday night we went back to the curfew and everyone obeyed it. Common sense and everyone won.

When you make a decision using your gut instincts, consider

asking yourself the following questions, using as much information that you have collected as possible.

- Which options capture my interest the most?
- Which options am I able to act on immediately?
- What further information do I need to make a decision?

Some people use how they physically feel when they receive the answers to questions like those above to tell them which option is best. Others may use their emotions as their intuitive guide by simply "feeling right" about a decision they've been wrestling with.

You will usually get the best and most helpful insight to making a decision if you ask questions that require more than yes-or-no answers. One method that helps to do this is writing information down. This simple action can help you achieve greater success in learning what your gut is trying to tell you. This technique is much like brainstorming.

To keep your gut instincts fine-tuned, keep the following rules in mind:

- *Stay with the work even if it bores you or floors you.* Understand that to do your best work you have to possess the facts. Obviously, you should perform further research using your computer or other backup materials if this is necessary. Feel comfortable—don't be afraid—to ask the people around you for their opinion and advice.
- *Changing your mind about a decision is okay, but keep a record of it.* It is important to have a record to which you can refer, listing the reasons for that change. That way, your change in position cannot be fairly described as a "flip-flop."
- *Give your intuition a chance to comment.* Again, marshal the facts, and when you review your thoughts give your muse—your intuition—the opportunity to speak. It will work almost every time, but not every time. So what! In baseball a .333 bat-

ting average is considered outstanding. That is one hit every three times at bat.

• *Do not adopt a position because it is considered safe and politically correct.* Have courage to advance a radical position that is rationally presented, especially if you believe in that proposition.

• *This, above all: To thine own self be true.* This is the cardinal rule for me. It is taken from William Shakespeare's tragic play *Hamlet,* when the character Polonius prepares his son Laertes for a long journey abroad and is facing the unknown.

Here is a generic definition of intuition: *direct and immediate knowledge that does not come from the rational side of the brain.* It tells you what you need to know, and when you need to know it. You can gain vital insight into yourself and your professional world when your instincts are fine-tuned because they are being used.

If you are having a tough time trusting your gut, consider using one of the following three tests developed by Harvard Business School professors.

1. *The Newspaper Test.* If your final decision were to appear on the front page of your local paper in the morning, what would the consequences be?

2. *The Golden Rule Test.* Walk a mile in the other person's shoes. How would you feel if your decision were enacted?

3. *The Best Friend Test.* Talk with people who know you well and respect you. They will understand your character and how the decision will affect you.

How I Use and Strengthen My Intuition

The following three areas are key to strengthening one's intuition:

1. *Organization.* Being organized is extremely helpful. Getting a lot done requires that you be organized so that you can organize others. I believe in the moderately cluttered desk, by which I mean having no more than two moderate-sized piles of papers on the desk: one pile for important papers in terms of priority of your time, and the second pile for items of lesser importance, where a delay in not responding for a week will not adversely affect the outcome or the attitude of those waiting for a response.

2. *Time Management.* I am proud of the fact that in addition to my working at Bryan Cave, where I am a member of the regulatory affairs, public policy, and legislative client service group, I have eight other jobs. I get them all done on time, and I am proud of my work product. Allocating your time is an important key to effectiveness. Some people may want to keep time sheets. I prefer relying on my memory and sense of organization to allocate time in a competent way.

3. *Practice, Practice, Practice.* When it comes to strengthening my intuition, to me there is no greater aid than practice: doing what I have described in this chapter, gathering the facts, and letting your muse take over.

MY NINE JOBS

1. I am a partner in the law firm Bryan Cave, LLP.
2. I host a weekly call-in show on Bloomberg Radio.
3. I am a weekly commentator on Bloomberg Radio.
4. I am a weekly guest on NY1 "Inside City Hall."
5. I write weekly political Commentaries.
6. I write movie reviews.
7. I lecture around the country.
8. I write books.
9. I appear in television commercials.

Chapter Eight

PICKING YOUR FIGHTS, ENFORCING YOUR RIGHTS

Many New Yorkers may remember the time when I was mayor and I made a big hullabaloo about the public transportation unions engaging in an illegal strike instead of continuing with collective bargaining. Under the state Taylor law, if collective bargaining failed, each side had the right to demand mandatory arbitration. The arbitrators could determine all aspects of the contract being bargained, including wage increases, and impose their determination upon the parties.

The illegal strike in 1980 went on for eleven days. Let me tell you how I devised our plan to fight the union and win.

The Transportation Workers Union (TWU) made demands that we did not think were fair or within the city's financial capacity. If we agreed to them, these demands would become the pattern for all 300,000 city employees in other unions, so I rejected them. The negotiations were conducted on behalf of management by the State of New York under Governor Hugh Carey, but the city was obviously involved because the city owns the subways and pay a substantial part of the costs, so my opinion and judgment counted.

When the TWU went on strike at midnight, I told my deputy mayors and the top commissioners that we would meet the next day at 5:00 A.M. in Police Commissioner Bob McGuire's office. When we gathered in his office, Bob said, "We can't run the trains and buses. If we tried, we would kill people. All I can do is control the street traffic and try to arrange car pools and expand parking."

As Bob was speaking, I looked out his office window on the 14th floor of the building that overlooked the Brooklyn Bridge, and I saw tens of thousands of people walking across the bridge. At that moment, it clicked in my mind how we would win this battle.

I said to Bob, "You continue to fill in everyone on the details. I'll be right back." I took the elevator to the ground floor where the press had gathered and walked with them at a rapid pace to the Brooklyn Bridge. When I got on the bridge, people began to applaud my presence. I responded with, "Keep walking. We are not going to let these bastards bring us to our knees." The applause got louder. And that was it.

Everyone viewed transportation strikes as incapable of being won by the city. In 1966, right at the beginning of John Lindsay's term as mayor, such a strike nearly destroyed his administration. He gave the strikers everything they wanted and lost enormous face and prestige with the public.

What I did during the eleven-day-strike was to go to the five bridges that connect Manhattan with the four other boroughs. I would go at 7:00 A.M. and encourage commuters to walk to work, and then I'd return at 5:00 P.M. and applaud them as they walked home.

We won. The union was so upset with our success in keeping the city going and getting people to work, they asked that their contract be extended in length for more than the scheduled two years. They did not want to be the first union the next time to have their contract come up for renewal and be the first in line to negotiate. They wanted to be last, and we obliged them.

Which Battles Are Worth Pursuing

A mayor is always involved in battles. Choosing the battle to which you apply all your strength depends on your resources. Those resources include your personal strength and mindset and the city's resources in terms of money and personnel. It is important to weigh the significance of the battle in terms of impact on the city and the willingness of its citizens to support you. The same applies to whatever battle you may be fighting, whether in politics or in business. Always assess your assets and goals.

Individuals often choose battles based on their core values and their resources available. These resources usually include time and finances. You can determine what your core values are by answering the three following questions:

1. *What do you value?* Walt Disney's nephew, Roy Disney, an American film executive, once said, "It is not hard to make decisions once you know what your values are." When you discover what is important to you and go after what you believe in, you will see which battles are worth pursuing.

2. *What is and is not worth fighting for?* Once you determine your values, you will know what battles you can remove from your list.

3. *Which issues and outcomes can you live with?* When you can see which conditions you can realistically accept, you will have an incredible sense of calmness, which will help you conserve energy for those battles you will fight for.

Some battles simply are not worth fighting for. If the battle is something you and others will not remember one year or even five years from now, it may not be worth your spending the energy and resources.

You can become a greater success in your business or campaign by knowing that you must be prepared to settle battles. Also, be prepared to avoid them where there is evidence that you have little or no chance of winning. But don't flinch in taking on an important battle even when the odds are somewhat against you. My rule is to take a chance on the outcome if you have a 40 percent chance of winning. If the odds are less than that, you should seriously consider settling.

For example, I was the Democratic District Leader of Greenwich Village from 1963 to 1966. At that time the Village, where I have lived since 1956, was the center of the city's cultural life. Young people from their teens to their thirties would walk the streets of the Village every night. The hub of activity was MacDougal Street in an Italian neighborhood, which ran for several blocks. Many coffee houses and entertainment places lined that street. The people who lived on MacDougal Street felt as though they were living in hell, particularly on weekends when the traffic and pedestrian noise increased and they were confronted with the antisocial behavior of some, such as those who would urinate in doorways and on the street.

Most of the people in that neighborhood were supporters of Carmine DeSapio, my political arch enemy. I held a public meeting and invited the neighborhood people to attend. Even Allen Ginsberg, the Village Beat poet, came. A new organization formed as a result of that meeting—the MacDougal Neighborhood Association known as MANA—and I was unanimously accepted as the leader.

As a group we counted the number of people who passed a particular store on a Saturday night during a one-hour period, and the number was 10,000. As a result of a lot of hard work, we changed the entire neighborhood. Bob Wagner, the city's mayor at the time, was a friend and political ally of mine. We pressured him to help, and today as a result of our actions that street is livable and has been for many years.

Some of the things we did included getting the tourist buses rerouted. But mainly we applied pressure to get more foot-patrol cops assigned to the area, with orders to give summons to or arrest those engaged in antisocial or criminal acts, such as urinating in public.

Sometimes Compromise Is the Best Strategy

As you are facing different issues, you need to determine whether to make a big deal about what it is you are doing, or simply just let it go. I typically choose to win my position by bringing lots of media and public attention to it, or I will compromise.

Case in point: When I was in the Congress, Richard Nixon left office before the U.S. Senate could take up his impeachment—which is comparable to an indictment by a grand jury. Gerald Ford, who then became president, chose Governor of New York Nelson Rockefeller to be his vice president. Rockefeller wanted his nomination to be confirmed by Congress and he wanted the African-American and Jewish congressional members from New York to vote for him. He had an emissary talk to me, asking for support.

For me, an important issue was then, and still is, the security of Israel. I told the emissary that Rockefeller's position on Israel was not sufficiently supportive, and I outlined measures that I believed he should publicly support. We negotiated over a period of days until it became clear that he had made his last concession. Feeling that was the case, I said, "Now I will vote for him," and I did.

After Rockefeller was confirmed, I stood in line at the Senate

Chamber to congratulate him. As I recall, when I reached him he said, "I'll never forget you." I never had cause to ask his support for anything, so I never tested him on that promise. But his public statements and support of Israel, as a result of my negotiating stance, were much better. I knew when to halt my demands, shake hands on agreement, and go on to the next issue.

It is important *you do not turn a disagreement into a moral issue, unless, of course, it is one. It is difficult to compromise on those kind of issues. Always see the dispute from the other side's vantage point, and be sure you have all the facts.*

Choosing how you will react to a situation is paramount in picking your battles and enforcing your rights. You can react in a more educated and peaceful way when you have all your facts—one strategy I would recommend more often than not.

At times you may have to make compromises in the battles you select. Some people usually consider the financial aspect at this point, since it is a resource. As a younger man with more vim and vigor, I was willing to fight more than now for the last point in any dispute. Now I accept more compromises.

Which brings up a good point. Everyone recognizes a difference in the actions of those who are young and those who have entered senior status. Today, seniors participate at work for longer periods of time, either formally or informally. I am now 82 years old. I have had a stroke, heart attack, and prostate problems, yet I continue to work every day. I mention this because I have tried to weigh how my responses to problems have changed. As an older man, and I hope a wiser one as a result of life's experiences, I think I am willing to be less self-righteous and more understanding of the other side's problems.

People may tell you *that you are right or wrong or try and change your resolve about which battles are worth fighting. My advice is to see their position from their perspective and tell them "You have a good point there." But you don't have to agree with them.*

How to Handle Conflict with Diplomacy

A good illustration of two people with totally different attitudes and positions on public matters is Mary Matalin and James Carville. Matalin was a senior advisor to Vice President Dick Cheney, worked with President George W. Bush, and has been involved with the Republican Party as long as I can remember. She is married to James Carville, a committed Democrat who ran many Democratic campaigns, including the successful campaigns of President Bill Clinton.

These two people often appear together on television programs offering different and generally opposite points of view. I believe their presentation is understandably intended to increase the viewing audience and to entertain audiences as a husband-and-wife team politically at war. While their arguments are strongly delivered, they always convey affection for one another, which is undoubtedly genuine. Even if you are not a husband and wife engaged in debate, always be courteous and don't interrupt the other person's statements. If they abuse you, point out that your responses to them have been courteous, rather than putting your opponent on trial like a district attorney.

Some people use the LCS strategy: like, concern, suggest. Find something you *like* about the other person's position, discuss and highlight your *concerns*, and then make a few good *suggestions*. Following this strategy respects the view points of the other party and maintains good communication.

Life is full of obstacles and conflicts. I believe the best way to deal with them is the obvious one—remove them. Where you can, rely on your strength and brain power. There are no extra points for doing it yourself, so always reach out to family, friends, or your support network for assistance. When it comes to conflict with others, decide for yourself where you will not compromise. Be careful to limit those no-compromise issues. Identify those issues on which you can completely fold and accept your opponent's position. Always try to convey courtesy and understanding—it will go a long way.

If, however, you are not able to remove the conflict, then the best way to manage the conflict is with good communication. This will help lead to a mutually agreeable solution by promoting a give-and-take open dialogue that focuses on the problem, not the emotion. Here are three ways to help manage conflict:

1. *Respect the viewpoints of others.* We all have difficult people in our lives, and they typically have different viewpoints from ours.

2. *Communicate without anger or sarcasm.* An example of how to do this would be, "I hear you and I understand your point, but for me this is the right principle. You are entitled to your opinion."

3. *Don't be a perfectionist.* Achieve your goal as much as you can. If it is reasonably close, consider what demanding total success may provide: failure. Be prudent and exercise common sense.

In dealing with conflict, let me suggest that you consider what I do:

- Get a good night's sleep before the battle begins.
- Organize your notes and study them. If at all possible, speak from memory rather than from your notes.
- Look directly into the eyes of your audience.
- Listen to what is said so that your follow-up question or response is on point and, hopefully, devastating. Do not take the role of district attorney vis-à-vis your opponent. People don't like that. They prefer the "nice guy" approach.

One of the great battles I supported relates to the New York City Gay Pride parade. When I was a congressman, I helped the parade organizers obtain a permit from the Parks Department allowing them to use Central Park. Very few people in public office at the time were willing to associate themselves with the parade. Today, many public officials, including current Mayor Michael Bloomberg and Senator Hillary Clinton, proudly lead that parade. It is one of New York City's great annual events, and gay and straight people from all over the United States come to New York to be a part of it.

A Final Word About Choosing Your Battles

Picking your fights and enforcing your rights is also about knowing when to admit you are wrong and acknowledging your mistakes. As Benjamin Franklin once said, "I haven't failed, I have had 10,000 ideas that didn't work."

We are all human and we all make mistakes. Accepting and admitting them is a major key to success. To stay with a point of view that deep in your heart you know is wrong is terribly counterproductive. Your opponents may lose respect for you, thinking that you are either stupid or a liar in continuing to mouth statements that you both know are wrong.

With the passage of time, you don't get smarter but you should get wiser. I think that has happened in my case, leading to a greater understanding of the needs of my opponents.

Again, it is important that you pick your battles. Sometimes you won't have the option and the battle will be thrust upon you. When you can choose, limit the number based on your capacity and resources. One battle at a time is best, but life generally provides a bumpy road, and you have to roll with the punches. A mixed metaphor, I know, but nevertheless true.

MY CURRENT ONGOING BATTLES

• *Confronting Terrorism.* Getting the American public to understand the battle of the century, which is the war of civilizations between the western "free" world and the Islamic world of terror, is at the top of my list of battles. The Islamic terrorists have stated what their values and goals include. They want to convert or kill us. Shocking but true.

Abu Musab al-Zarqawi, a former major Al-Qaeda leader in Iraq, laid it out clearly for us, just like Adolf Hitler did in *Mein Kampf*. Before al-Zarqawi was killed by an American bomb, he issued a letter in which he wrote, "Killing the infidels is our religion, slaughtering them is our religion, until they convert to Islam or pay us tribute." My fear is that western civilization is unwilling to fight the terrorists who love death and martyrdom, while we treasure life. Are we willing to pay the costs and casualties of war? I'm not sure that we are, but I am sure this war of civilizations will go on for at least thirty more years.

• *Developing Alternative Fuel Sources.* A major battle we should all join in is ending our dependence on oil and creating alternatives to fossil fuel. It can be done, but not simply by mouthing supportive words. In my judgment, we need a Manhattan Project like we had when we developed the nuclear bomb in World War II. The cost of that project was $2 billion, which translated into true dollars today would be $21 billion. That's not very much money. Yet the Congress and the President have so far refused to take the measures needed to create a Manhattan Project for fuel alternatives.

• *The Race for President.* Politically, I am supporting Hillary Clinton for president, and I believe she can win. I have publicly announced I am a soldier in her army. I need to support politicians who advance the positions and causes of the middle class, and I have done so all my political life. I believe many more politicians now accept those middle-class values.

Chapter Nine

TURNING MISTAKES INTO OPPORTUNITIES

From a public career point of view, the greatest
mistake I ever made was running for a State Assembly seat from
Greenwich Village. The seat had been held for years by William
Passanante, who was the candidate of the regular organization
in the Village, known as the Tamawa Democratic Club. This
club was led by the Manhattan County Leader, Carmine De-
Sapio. Although not a reform candidate, Passanante was quite
liberal on issues like abortion and gay rights, which back in
1962 were very controversial.

The Village Independent Democrats (VID) Club was formed
in 1956 in order to support the candidacy of Adlai Stevenson,
who was running for president for a second time. After he had
lost to Dwight Eisenhower, the club continued. We decided that
we would contest every possible position at every level with the
old-line club called Tamawa, which included candidates for
public office, judicial positions, and the key position of Democratic District Leader. The latter position was held by Carmine
DeSapio, who was also the head of Tammany Hall, the New
York County Democratic Organization.

No one from our club stepped forward to run for the Assembly, so I decided to run. When I lost that election, receiving only 42 percent of the votes, I told my several hundred supporters at the club, "Politics is a dirty business. I will never run again." I felt betrayed by two leading members of the Democratic Party: Mayor Robert F. Wagner and U.S. Senator Herbert Lehman. They supported Passanante, even though they both were leaders of the Reform Movement formed to take the Democratic Party away from the old-liners like Carmine DeSapio, the biggest "boss" in town.

After thinking long and hard about that election, I realized how wrong I had been to run against Passanante, because I knew very little about city or state government. As a result of that loss, however, I studied government and became an expert. Losing that election for the Assembly seat eventually led to my running for the City Council, Congress, and finally the mayoralty, and winning all three offices.

The moral of the story for me was that it was important to recognize why I lost. This is an essential rule for anyone who has lost an election, a promotion, a contract, or a job. Losing prepares you for your next opportunity, if you take some time to examine the reasons why you lost. Of the twenty-three elections in which I was a candidate, I lost three and won twenty— sometimes a primary, a run-off, and a general election all within the same year.

Learn from Your Mistakes

In assessing what went wrong, it is critical that you be totally honest with yourself and accept responsibility where appropriate.

The message is simple: Learn from your mistakes. I have continuously referred to one of my core beliefs, "Be Not Afraid." Do not be afraid to accept responsibility and learn from your mistakes.

Everyone makes mistakes, and everyone can recover from them, except when the mistakes involve criminal acts. For the most part, those kinds of acts are nearly impossible to recover from, especially for someone seeking public office.

I have found the most common error is engaging in loose language, offering an opinion on a subject where you really don't have the facts. That also involves stating something you think is obviously true, but which can turn people off or can blow up in your face when it turns out not to be true.

I made this particular mistake when I was invited by John Cardinal O'Connor to join him and others on a pilgrimage to Ireland. While I was there, I was asked by an American reporter, Tony Guida, about Ireland's "troubles" and the role of the British. I offered the opinion that the British soldiers stationed in Northern Ireland were "peacekeepers." I said they were separating the contestants in the civil war between the Protestants and the Catholics. I also said that they had tried to end discrimination against Catholics in jobs and housing.

My interview was broadcast around the world and caused an uproar. Catholics were indignant that I had said nice things about the British. For their part, the Brits were very effusive in their praise of me, and along with Prime Minister Margaret Thatcher and members of the House of Commons, they celebrated my congratulatory language. On my return to New York City, I was walking behind the Cardinal in the airport, and I overheard him being interviewed by a reporter asking for his opinion of what I had said. He replied, "They were the dumbest comments I have heard in a long time."

When I arrived at City Hall, a number of my staff members expressed their distress with my comments. I said, "But I thought it was true that the British had tried to make amends for their earlier behavior." One of the commissioners, who is a good friend of mine said, "But mayor, how can you equate 800 years of oppression with three years of trying to do the right thing?" I immediately realized that he was right. I spent the next three months meeting with Irish groups. They first voiced their disappointment for my having said that the British were "peace-keepers," and then they'd convey that they forgave me because they knew I held the Irish in such high regard.

Making a mistake is not bad *unless you keep making the same one over and over again. Analyze what you've done wrong and, depending on the situation, determine your responsibility. It is much better to learn from your mistakes by admitting it was your fault. If you do not hold yourself responsible, then you have learned nothing.*

In my 1981 and 1985 mayoral reelection campaigns, the Irish and Italians gave me 81 percent of their vote, while the Jews (and I am Jewish, as you may know) only gave me 73 percent of their support. The explanation was, I believe, that I wasn't liberal enough, that indeed I was too conservative. My description of myself in every election going back as far as 1973 added to their frustration. I describe myself as a "liberal with sanity." What's the moral here? If you establish firm and deep roots with a group of people, such as an ethnic or religious community, you can count on loyalty ultimately coming to the fore even if for a few passing moments you make a mistake that results in the group being upset, distressed, or even angry.

It was important, however, that I admitted error. I didn't

grovel nor did they want me to. But everyone admires the person who after taking a position admits error and provides the reasons why the error was committed. My own belief and practice on getting involved in controversial matters is to not take polls. Do not weigh the consequences when truth, substance, or conscience is involved. If you do what you think is right and honorable, then it's okay to poll and see if your instinct was right on target.

If you have made a mistake, admit it. *Don't try to hide it. If you do, it will eventually come out and the consequences will be worse in the long run.*

Mistakes on the Job

To those of you who have been fired from a job, I urge you to examine why. Be honest with yourself and your job performance. If you didn't enjoy your job, you should have quit long before being fired. If you feared the consequences of quitting, such as losing your salary, be appreciative that the decision was made for you. Remember, you spend more time on the job than doing anything else.

That being said, the best advice I can give in this regard is to learn as much as you can about your chosen field: Become an expert. In most cases, the better you are at a job and the more you know about it, the happier you will be with that job. When you're struggling to understand your job or simply cannot do it well, every day is an unpleasant grind.

My mother used to say that it is easier to find a new job while still working at your old one, which is true. But even then, at some point you have to decide when it is time to quit. If you stay, your entire persona will suffer.

Mistakes in Public Office

It is also important to note that while people in politics have their share of engaging in criminality, but on the whole, I believe it is fair to say there is a winnowing system in politics that drives the corrupt politician out of office faster than in any other job. Those are elections. Your adversary is constantly looking to expose you, and law enforcement officials pay a lot of attention to public officials. So I have come to the conclusion that elected public officials are, for the most part, more honest than the society from which they come. Nevertheless, too many public officials violate their trust and fiduciary relationships with the electorate. They often pay tougher penalties than those in other professions because the public is so outraged, and judges recognize that anger when it comes to sentencing.

Wise people admit their mistakes easily. *Not-so-wise people repeat the same mistakes over and over.*

If you think you may have foolishly committed a breach of ethics or possibly have committed a crime, seek the advice of someone who is knowledgeable. Not everyone is. My advice is to consult an attorney. And remember, you get what you pay for, so unless you are consulting a relative or friend, expect to pay for that advice. And get it early on before you dig yourself in deeper and perhaps court further trouble. The worst part of any situation is the cover-up, which can be far worse than any action you may have taken. Seeking early advice will hopefully prevent a cover-up.

Turning Mistakes into Opportunities

You have to ask yourself several questions about the best way to handle mistakes. Before you can turn a mistake into an opportunity, you have to define the mistake.

Was it something you did not think through? If that is the case, you have to reexamine your thought process. Perhaps there is something you overlooked and you were too quick to reach a decision and did not perform adequate due diligence. Too often, you may not have asked the definitive question that might have cleared up any confusion.

Of course, there is always the question—was it really a mistake? Maybe there were outside influences beyond your control.

You will create buzz when people see that you readily accept responsibility when you make a mistake. But you will create even more buzz when you show that you have learned from your mistakes—that you have gained experience.

You cannot be afraid of taking chances as a way of avoiding mistakes. Too many people get too comfortable in a routine, and do not want to change. They have been "successful" doing things their way, and therefore they do not see why they should change. You can just as easily make a mistake by maintaining the status quo as by trying something new.

Then, there are others who change too often, who repeatedly bend with the wind, foolishly thinking they can't be caught making a mistake. You must not lose your courage. Constant shifting—often called flip-flopping—to keep from making mistakes will make others lose confidence in you—and you will still make mistakes along the way. Again, there's nothing wrong with making a mistake and changing your position. Just explain why.

God has given each of us pluses and minuses. It's not all about our DNA, although that does account for much of our character and personality. Genes often determine outcomes. Nevertheless, even when life is stacked against you, I believe you can change the odds or outcome by your willingness to learn and sacrifice in the search for excellence. Be willing to accept the premise that lemons can be turned into lemonade. It takes a person totally honest with himself or herself to make the needed changes.

Part Four

RECOGNIZING VICTORY

I have been privileged to experience the pleasure of many victories during my eighty-two years of life. I have also experienced the pain of defeats which, fortunately, were far less in number and impact.

As a child, I always thought I would be a lawyer. As I've mentioned before, I was not an athletic kid and did not do well in sports, although I tried. My older brother Harold was a terrific athlete, and I longed to be as good as he was. He told me to use my talents of public speaking. And that's what I did.

1. This book will help you lay out the ways and means for those who want to advance and be successful in creating buzz in their careers.

2. Recognizing your victories is an important part of creating buzz. If you don't know when you have succeeded, it's unlikely that anyone else will do it for you.

Chapter Ten

STAYING ORGANIZED

What does staying organized have to do with creating buzz? It is an essential ingredient. When you are able to focus on the task at hand and keep moving forward to accomplish your goals, others start to notice. They come to trust you and your ability to get things done.

During World War II, I served in the 104th Combat Infantry Division, known as the Timberwolves. I believe my mind became most focused during that time. Combat certainly focuses your mind on survival. No truer statement was ever made than, "There are no atheists in foxholes."

I was able to lead an interesting life as a private-sector lawyer for about twenty years, and then in the public sector for the next twenty years. I served as a city councilman, congressman, and then as mayor. In 1990 I once again returned to the private sector to practice law. With luck, I'll be at this job for at least ten more years.

Every morning my alarm clock goes off at 5 A.M. I reach for the envelope that contains my daily schedule, and based on what's in store, I select my suit and tie. Some argue that a red tie is no longer considered a power tie, but I still believe it is.

Three days a week—Monday, Wednesday, and Friday—I exercise with a personal trainer for one hour at the gym one block from my office. By 8:30 A.M. I'm in the office and work until 4:00 P.M. Afterward, I typically go home. On Tuesdays and Thursdays, when I don't go to the gym, I get to the office at 7:30 A.M. and start my day at the law office earlier.

Most of Monday is spent preparing my weekly Commentary and movie reviews, which I write in longhand over the weekend and edit at the office once they are typed. Here at the Bryan Cave law firm, where I am a partner, I am a member of the regulatory affairs, public policy, and legislation client service group. During the day, I'll advise clients on matters relating to city, state, and other governmental issues. The remainder of my day is spent on correspondence, writing speeches, participating in TV and radio interviews, and reading the newspapers in preparation for my weekly radio and television programs.

Being organized, understanding the need for sleep, going to the gym three times a week, and eating healthy food are absolutely essential to my overall success. Some people will succeed without being organized, getting enough sleep, or eating a healthy diet, but they really are few and far between.

I am also fortunate to have two wonderful assistants: Jody Smith and Mary Garrigan. They exercise superb, independent judgment, get things done in a timely manner, and make it possible for me to meet by deadlines.

People range from being very sloppy *and disorganized to being so organized that they become prisoners to their own schedule. The way to create a balance in your life is to decide what your strengths and weaknesses are and to know that your* *strengths will protect you and that you must guard against your weaknesses. This is a view I practice often.*

How I Organized New York City

One way I have organized my life, my objectives, and my future has been to rely on the Catholic hymn "Be Not Afraid," to which I have referred many times throughout this book. It has been of enormous help to me throughout the years. As mayor, I was always being tested and always on the firing line. By staying organized and keeping an eye on my goals, no matter what obstacles arose, I was able to persevere.

Few people thought I could win the position of mayor, but I knew that if I could get out my message, I could do it. My message was my belief in middle-class values. I knew that most people wanted to be considered middle class and that the poor often believed and stated they were middle class, even when they were not in terms of income.

My responsibility as mayor escalated with each passing year. Remember, New York City's budget is the fourth largest in the country. First in size is the U.S. budget, followed by the budgets of the State of California, the State of New York, and then New York City. When I was in office, seven million people lived in the city. The number today is eight million, and it is estimated that within twenty years it will increase to nine million.

When I became mayor, a state law was enacted requiring that I balance the city's budget in four years. During the first three years, I could borrow money to keep the city going, as long as someone was willing to lend it to us. If the budget was not bal-

In New York City, the tendency of most candidates is either to be or try to convey they are progressive —more liberal than liberal. Not me. Early on I referred to myself as "a liberal with sanity." My announcing that I was a liberal with sanity made my job as a mayor much easier. I was able to say to the many progressives who didn't care that the city was on the edge of bankruptcy that the days of handing out money borrowed from the banks for good or bad purposes was over. As for you, you must determine where you fit in that enormous range from arch-conservative to arch-liberal and everything in between.

anced in the fourth year, I would be a failure and the city would have to file for bankruptcy.

The operating budget during my first year as mayor was about $14 billion. The city borrowed about $1 billion a year to finance the budget. Over the four years my responsibility was to gradually reduce the expenditures in order to balance the budget. But there was a problem. Two-thirds of our operating budget was overwhelmingly spent on the poor in providing services like education, police, sanitation, as well as all the services provided under the title of human resources, including food, jobs, and hospital and medical services. So those who suffered the most when the budget was cut were the poor.

The long and short of it was that if we went into bankruptcy, we would become another Detroit and the poor would suffer and have no future. I couldn't let that happen. To organize the city I had to ultimately balance the budget, and today every mayor is required to do the same. As a result, the city is once again a financial colossus and the international capital of finance, commerce, culture, and communication.

Here is the organization plan I implemented:

1. Reduce the workforce. This reduced the city's expenditures, plain and simple.

2. Reduce the services, such as the number of sanitation pick-ups, and reduce personnel, such as the number of police on the force. The highest number of cops during my administration was 28,000, and the lowest number after attrition was 22,000. The city population suffered, but ultimately it was worth it.

3. Prepare a financial plan, which is accepted by the financial institutions and which will move the city toward a balanced budget. This plan must be published each year.

That balanced budget began during the third year of my administration and has been continued by every mayor since.

Not knowing the resolve of any future mayor, the Legislature of the State of New York established a Financial Control Board with the power to overrule the mayor and the City Council on financial matters. Some might have been frightened or resentful of such a Board, but I was not. I always publicly stated that I was tougher than any Financial Board and ahead of them on any financial issue. At the same time, I would say to the municipal union leaders, "You better do what I tell you to do or I will bring in the Financial Control Board and God knows what they will do to you."

To implement a plan like this, mayors or anyone in this role have to be prepared for negative reactions. Those same pressures and powers are directed at anyone in charge of budgeting. You need the inner strength to take the brickbats and the epithets that will be hurled at you, which happened to me at public meetings or when I walked the streets in poverty areas. But in the end, if your actions are correct, people will recognize what you have done to help them, and they will thank you.

Being organized *allows you to keep to your schedule. If you determine and rate your priorities and manage your time properly, you will be able to mold and organize your life, career, and future.*

How I Stay Organized Today

Today I have many tasks, which I listed earlier. For your convenience, let me summarize them again here. I am a practicing lawyer. I write weekly movie reviews and a weekly Commentary on issues of the day, from the Iraq war and illegal immigration to medical care. I have a weekly radio and television show. I also write books and have many speaking engagements in the United States and abroad. I have never missed a deadline and attribute my success to the organization of my daily efforts and to my superb staff.

Here are a few key ideas that help me handle my many separate tasks and stay organized every day:

1. *Listen to your inner voice.* I learned that my brain continues to function even while I am sleeping. Many times when I am searching exhaustively for the answer to a perplexing problem, I will dream about it and suddenly know what has to be done.

I hear a silent voice telling me that I will remember everything in the morning but I know I won't, so I force myself to waken, reach for the pad on my bedside table, and jot down the solution.

2. *Keep track.* Every day I assess the output need for that day as well as the balance of the week. I never allow myself to be overcome by a feeling that there is too much to do. I know that if I apply myself it will get done, even if at the end of the week I feel exhausted. You must always feel obligated to fulfill your commitments.

3. *Write things down.* I do something that I don't believe enough people do. I carry a small pad with me and jot down things to be done when they occur to me. Those items remain on my list until I can check them off as either having been completed or in the process of being done. As I mentioned above, I also place that notepad next to my bed in case an idea occurs to me during the night.

4. *Be ready for anything.* Being—and remaining—organized helps you be prepared for the unexpected. Life is filled with unexpected twists and turns, so having a schedule helps you deal with whatever comes up. Forget any worries that may arise from tasks or responsibilities that may impede your ability to stay organized. Focus on the problems you can overcome by simply addressing and solving them.

5. *Stick to your passions.* Keep in mind that our best results occur when we are engaged in labors of love. So pick your work opportunities carefully. If you find that you are bored, uninterested, or not proficient in what you are doing, it will have a negative impact on your schedule. Look for another career opportunity.

Part of staying organized *requires you to prioritize your life. Money is important, particularly if you have family obligations, but it should not be your most important goal. Keep in mind that your desire to succeed at your particular goals may mean suffering a little today to ensure success at a later time.*

My Life Is Organized in Archives

Over the years I have accumulated a vast collection of official papers from my City Council, Congressional and mayoral days. All of my files, including my non-legal files since returning to the private sector seventeen years ago, are housed at LaGuardia Community College's La Guardia and Wagner Archives. When the Archives received my public papers in 1990, I was told they ran 4,100 linear feet, double the volume of the files of Mayors LaGuardia and Wagner in the aggregate. My files are now listed on the Archives' website at www.laguardiawagnerarchive.lag cc.cuny.edu.

Those files are described by the Archives as consisting of:

- Microfilm copies of my departmental correspondence and other documents, representing 4,000 folders of my mayoral papers held by the Municipal Archives.
- Several years of my radio Commentaries in html/PDF format that are available on the website, along with general correspondence and letters to the editor, which are accessible to researchers in electronic format (MS Word) at the Archives.

- More than 1,000 photographs, from my days as an Army private (later, sergeant) in World War II to the present.
- Access on the website to photographs of about 270 artifacts belonging to me.
- Nearly 2,000 videos—mostly recordings of me on TV broadcasts—and seventy oral histories recounting the "Koch administration years."

From articles to clippings to administration and congressional files, it is all there and is all organized.

Maintain a Good Staff

One of the most important keys to staying organized is to enlist the help of others. Many leaders in business and politics create buzz with the quality of the people who serve under them. You look good when you hire good people. You look bad when you hire incompetent people or those who will just rubberstamp every decision you make. I have always insisted on having the best people on my staff.

I am intolerant of inefficiency, yet I understand mistakes. I told the commissioners in my mayoral administration that I would protect and defend them if they stumbled and made a mistake or if they embarked on an experimental course of action that failed, provided they had used common sense. I didn't want them to not try new approaches to problems out of fear of failing.

As I have mentioned, don't be unwilling to experiment for fear of failing, as long as you follow the rule of common sense. And make sure your staff knows you will stand by them if they take a chance and fail. Reasonable people will conclude that although a program may have failed, it made sense at the time

> **In difficult times** I would comfort myself with the thought that the voters elected me because they thought I was the best person for the job. I will give them my best, I thought —which I always did—and beyond that it is in the hands of God. Being organized is essential because of the shortness of time available to accomplish so many tasks.

to think it would work, and it was worth a try. So I repeat: Under those circumstances, you should stand up for and defend the people who tried.

I believe your DNA *often determines whether you will be a good manager. If you are not a good manager but are a policy person, you can still prevail by hiring the best people to work on your staff to address the issues with you.*

When you select your staff, look for people who seem to share your aspirations and motivations. You will know within the first thirty days whether they do. If they don't, fire them, no matter how difficult it may be. Second chances rarely work. If you keep them for more than thirty days, you will come to like them and know them better. It will be more difficult to get rid of them.

Chapter Eleven

HOW TO WITHSTAND PUBLIC SCRUTINY

Creating buzz is a key to achieving success, and it certainly has helped me along the way. However, a significant degree of public scrutiny comes with the territory. This is not always pleasant—whether you are in politics or business—but you must learn how to withstand it through your own personal honesty and integrity. Otherwise, you can find yourself fighting against negative buzz, and that can be a hard battle to win.

When you enter the political realm, you give up some of the normal privacy protections that most people enjoy. Public officials and those engaged in political matters can be slandered and libeled, but they are unable for the most part to collect damages, under a decision by the U.S. Supreme Court in a case known as *New York Times v. Sullivan, 1964.*

Most people familiar with that rule believe it was created to protect newspapers from being subject to a major money judgment for having libeled a southern law enforcement official involved in the civil rights battles of the Reverend Martin Luther King, Jr. The *Times* defamation involved an uncomplimentary description of the Montgomery, Alabama, police department's actions vis-à-vis Reverend King. The police department was under the command of Police Commissioner L.B. Sullivan, who sued for defamation.

The new rule provided that for the defendant to be held liable in such a situation, the public figure would have to show malice on the part of the defendant. In this case, the normal definition of malice—ill will—did not apply. The court's "actual malice" standard required that the plaintiff in a defamation or libel case prove that the publisher of the statement in question knew that the statement was false or acted in reckless disregard of its truth or falsity. The purpose of this decision was to protect the media from being financially destroyed because of bona fide, albeit false, efforts to keep the public informed. It is still possible to sue in such cases and to get a judgment against a defendant who is slandering or libeling you, but without an award of damages. So today, under the rule promulgated in the case of *New York Times v. Sullivan,* the media will on occasion publish false, libelous material without being held responsible.

Many people in public life fear the media and generally dislike reporters asking questions, but I do not. To be candid, I enjoy the verbal jousting.

Unreasonable Inquiries

Alternative newspapers have sprung up all over the country. Often their reporters make an effort to inquire about the sex lives of public officials and public figures. The issue recently arose in an interview that Wolf Blitzer of CNN had with Vice President Dick Cheney. Cheney's daughter, Mary, who by her own choice is a publicly identified lesbian, having written a book on her life discussing her same-sex companion, was artificially impregnated in order to have a baby. The vice president was asked about the criticism of right-wing groups to babies being born to and raised by two parents of the same gender. Cheney told Blitzer that his question was "over the line." I don't think the question was over the line, since Mary Cheney has written a book discussing her sexual orientation. When you make a point of your sexual orientation in public discussion, others surely have a right to make their comments and opinions known. But I believe the vice president was right not to respond.

On the other hand, when Andrew Sullivan decided to "out" me and two women in President Clinton's cabinet, I was outraged. In a December 1999 *New York Times Magazine* column titled "Not a Straight Story," Sullivan wrote, "In Clinton's cabinet, almost everyone is married or divorced, but for two who aren't, Donna Shalala and Janet Reno, their orientations are shrouded in deep ambiguity."

Sullivan went on, "In a recent issue of *New York Magazine* devoted to 'singles,' former New York Mayor Ed Koch was invited to write his own personals ad. This is what he wrote: 'White Male, 70-something former CEO and practicing attorney . . . Have belatedly concluded that everyone, straight or gay, needs a partner in life. How'm I doing?' What on earth are we supposed to make of that? Surely no heterosexual wanting to find a partner in a personals ad would feel the need to conceal the sex of the person he is looking for. Why? Koch could have refused to join in the magazine's game, retaining complete privacy, or he could have written an ad clearly looking for a woman. Instead, he chose to play Kinda Ask, Sorta Tell."

In my *Newsday* column that appeared December 24, 1999, in response to Sullivan's article, I wrote, "There are two kinds of outers: one, the homophobic heterosexual; and the other, the self-hating homosexual. Both are no different from the Jew-catchers of Nazi Germany. Having reached the age of 75 years [in 1999], I am flattered by any interest in my sexuality. But I am truly offended by the assaults on the privacy of the women . . . referred to in the article. They have done nothing to deserve his venom . . . I believe an individual's sexual orientation is a private matter. I have declined to discuss mine because it is no one's business. If someone denounces homosexuality and is himself a homosexual, then revealing that hypocrisy is reasonable . . . I have never denounced homosexuality or heterosexuality." Indeed, I believe homosexuals should have every right provided to heterosexuals, including the right to marry and adopt children.

Irrespective of the truth or falsity of the statements on sexual orientation, I believe Sullivan was wrong to make them. His reporting that the two women were unmarried was ridiculous. I pointed out there was no question that Oscar Wilde was homosexual, and he was married with two children. I believe a closeted homosexual or lesbian should only be identified or "outed" if that person has publicly attacked other gays and lesbians or supported anti-gay legislation. Those allegations could not accurately be made against me or Clinton's two female cabinet members. I don't believe any person should be required to answer a question about his or her sexuality. It's nobody's business and, indeed, the question is over the line.

As I have said, I have never denounced homosexuality or heterosexuality. In 1962, I ran for the New York State Assembly urging the repeal of the sodomy laws. In 1974, I was one of two New York members of Congress, the other being the late Bella Abzug, who sponsored a national gay rights bill. At that time, only three other members of Congress supported that bill.

In 1978, in one of my first acts as mayor of the City of New York, I issued an executive order prohibiting discrimination in government based on sexual orientation. In 1986, I signed a local law, the passage of which I had urged for many years, that prohibited discrimination in the private sector based on sexual orientation.

In my twelfth book, *I'm Not Done Yet*, I say:

I'm well aware of the occasional speculation, but it doesn't matter to me whether people think I'm straight or gay . . . Life is gentler and more comforting when you have someone to share it with. In my case it wasn't meant to be, although it is only lately that I find myself reflecting on it. I honestly didn't think about it much when I was younger, but I do now.

To Sullivan, I say: "I am disappointed by your speculation." To the *New York Times*, I say: "On this occasion you failed to live up to the motto established by your brilliant publisher, Adolph S. Ochs: 'All the News That's Fit to Print.'" To both the *Times* and Sullivan, I say: "You owe two fine public servants, Donna Shalala and Janet Reno, an apology."

Your Words Will Be Examined

Most important in dealing with the press is never to run away. Answer questions honestly or decline to respond when you think the question is inappropriate. Declining to comment might occasionally result in embarrassment, but in the long run it won't cause a problem. Do not engage in a cover-up. Many people have learned the hard way that it's the cover-up that gets you in trouble.

Understand that if you are in the big leagues, what you have said over the years, including the e-mails you have sent, is retrievable and will be examined. If you have been foolish in your utterances, you will pay a price. Remember, there is no off-the-record statement, no matter what the reporter says. If what you have said is worth reporting, the reporter may get your statement out to the public, if not in his own name then under someone else's byline.

Smart people can make terrible errors. Early in 2007, when Senator Joseph Biden (D-Del) announced that he was running for president, he referred to an African-American senator from Illinois, Barack Obama, who is also running for president. Biden said, "I mean, you got the first mainstream African-American who is articulate and bright and clean and a nice-looking guy . . . I mean, that's a storybook, man."

Biden's comments were intended to single out the senator and praise him, but his language deprecated every other African-American in public life by saying in effect that they were not "clean" or "nice-looking." Not even Jesse Jackson, Shirley Chisholm, or Al Sharpton, all of whom ran for president. Biden later explained that he meant "fresh thinking." So be careful and choose your words wisely.

I know that on many occasions I made foolish and indeed stupid statements. With me it was likely that I was trying to be funny and failed. So it was in 1982 when I ran for governor. I had previously described upstate New Yorkers as wasting their time in pickup trucks driving twenty miles to buy a gingham dress or a Sears Roebuck suit.

It was hubris that caused me to run for governor in 1982. It was hubris that caused newly elected Governor Eliot Spitzer to say to an assemblyman, "Listen, I'm a fucking steamroller, and I'll roll over you and anybody else." Hubris can turn you into a bully and severely damage your reputation. As they say, pride goeth before a fall. On the other hand, Spitzer's tactics seem to be working for him and have brought him unexpected successes. He may very well be the exception to the rule. I believe he is good for New York State and has a great future.

Let Honesty and Integrity Be Your Guides

You can be severely injured by the acts of those with whom you are associated. As I mentioned earlier, when I was mayor, a corruption scandal took place in a city agency involving Queens Borough President Donald Manes and Bronx Democratic Leader Stanley Friedman, neither of whom I had appointed. In fact, I got the Legislature to abolish Stanley Friedman's lifetime job as a member of the City's Board of Water Supply. I was in no way involved in their crimes; nevertheless, I went into a state of depression worrying that people might think I was. The prosecutor, Rudolph Giuliani, told a public meeting that I was not in any way involved with the corruption. Giuliani said:

> *I think I know as much about these investigations as anyone knows, including a lot of confidential material, and there's not a single shred of evidence or suggestion that Mayor Koch knew of crimes that were being committed by several of the Democratic leaders and the borough presidents, or had any involvement in those crimes, or would have done anything other than turn them in if he had found out about them.*

I was told by Howard Rubenstein, the head of one of the best-known public relations firms and who had advised Mayor Abe Beame, that I escaped public censure because of my reputation for personal integrity, which was universally accepted. He further stated that very few people could have survived the scandal.

The most comforting call that I received during those trying days was from John Cardinal O'Connor, with whom I was very friendly and with whom I had written a book, *His Eminence and Hizzoner.* The Cardinal called to say he knew I was depressed and that I shouldn't be because everyone knew I was an honest man. When I thanked him, he said, "Don't thank me, it is true." I replied, "Your Eminence, you called me; the Lubavitcher Rebbe did not call."

The Catholic chaplain of the police department, Msgr. John Kowski, said to me, "Mayor, can I talk to you frankly?"

Trembling internally, not knowing what he would say, I said, "Yes, Monsignor." He replied, "I mean totally candid." I replied, "Of course, Monsignor." He then said, "Fuck 'em," undoubtedly referring to the newspaper editorials denouncing me for the fact that these two men were friends of mine and had committed their chicanery on my watch. Those near-daily editorials and articles caused my depression. I shall always recall Msgr. Kowski and his words with great comfort and satisfaction.

If you lead an honest life and others do not, I believe there is a God who will protect you as He did me. And people like Cardinal O'Connor and Msgr. Kowski will help you get through enormously trying periods with their comforting words.

It is important to tell the truth. If you decline to respond to a question, you should state why. You need not volunteer the truth, simply because you know something the reporter does not know. You can with honor remain silent on the subject. There are, however, two situations when you can lie and have no regrets. One is when someone is dying of cancer. To comfort them I believe it is okay to say, "No, you don't have cancer, you only have jaundice, and you are getting well." That is what we told my mother, but I think she really knew.

The second situation, as I have already said, is when you fire someone. It is okay to say that he or she resigned to do other things, so as not to injure their career, unless they are being fired for criminality.

The Buzz Goes On

In a Commentary some time ago, I had voiced concern that the attacks and invectives used against President Bush by those opposed to his standing up to Islamic terrorism in Iraq might affect his spirit. On January 31, 2007, the president came to New York City to address an audience of about 200 people, of which I was one. It took place at the Sub-Treasury Building at Wall and Nassau Streets, where George Washington took the oath of office as our first president.

On the plane to New York with the president were several members of the New York Congressional Delegation, one of whom was Peter King, a good friend of mine. When Peter saw me in the auditorium, he said that on the plane he told the president of my concern and the president said to those flying with him, "My mother is worried, too." When President Bush began his speech he noted my presence saying, "And it's good to see my buddy, Mayor Ed Koch. Mr. Mayor, thank you for coming. Appreciate you being here." He delivered an excellent speech, particularly citing gains to the economy. When he finished he came down to shake hands. When he got to me, he pulled me forward, pressed his right cheek against my right cheek and whispered in my ear, "Don't worry about me. I'm okay."

I thought to myself, what a wonderful country. Here I am, a former kid from the Bronx, engaged in an intimate conversation with the president of the United States and he refers to me as a friend of his. The next day I was surprised to see that a photographer had captured that moment, and a photo of his greeting me appeared on the front page of the *New York Times* above the fold. God is good, and what happened is the best of buzz.

Chapter Twelve

BEING OPEN TO CHANGE

As you've seen, creating buzz starts with being true to yourself and your core beliefs, but that doesn't mean you should never change or forego new ways of doing things. Resistance to all change eventually will result in negative buzz, as people come to see you as stubborn and inflexible.

Situations change, perspectives change, and smart people know when they, too, must change. You should never announce a change just to take advantage of shifting conditions or opinion polls, but when you recognize the real need for change, embrace it and get out in front of it. Being open to change is a hallmark of leadership. It marks you as someone to listen to, someone to follow, and it gives you the most positive kind of buzz.

I underwent a change in philosophy after I changed jobs. When I served in Congress for nine years, I was rated by liberal groups as 100 percent in their corner. When I became mayor of New York City, I changed. I was seen as more conservative, but not as much as some people think. But I recognized the change and trumpeted it. People asked me to explain. I told them that, in Congress, if you presented me with a bill that promised to do good things for people, you had my vote. My record in Congress reflected that. I never asked how the new or additional services would be paid for. It was as though that was someone else's responsibility, not mine. My responsibility was only to do good things and leave to others how to pay for it.

When I was elected mayor, I found out that those good things I voted for were very expensive, and they had to be paid for, in many cases, by the locality. In this case, it was New York City. The city was broke—on the edge of bankruptcy—when I assumed office in 1978.

After I had been mayor for a year or two, I was discussing my change in philosophy. I said that if I could, I would sentence every member of Congress to serve one year as mayor as punishment for all of the financial pain they had caused the city and every other city in America.

I also said that my support for substantive matters affecting the people, particularly the poor, remained the same, except that in introducing or accepting a new program, I would want to know how it would be paid for. I wrote a Commentary at the time, called "The Mandate Millstone." It listed all the programs forced on cities where the Congress mandated that the cities pay all or the major costs. President Reagan referenced it in a footnote in his State of the Union address in 1982.

The desire of many in Washington to press for and impose new and good programs on the country, without regard to cost or how they will be paid for, still continues today. One of the largest federal mandates on the states and cities is President Bush's education program, known as the "No Child Left Behind" Act. The cost of the program is quite high and it is the cities and states that bear most of the costs.

I believe the people of the United States are fundamentally moderate in their beliefs, with moderate conservatives and moderate liberals holding the biggest blocks of votes. But I am not limiting this thinking to politics only. I believe you can apply this need for and use of moderation to anything you do, and you will stand out, be the center of the room, the center of discussion. Yes, radicalism makes a bigger splash, but only for a shorter time. Moderation can hold its own.

Also note that positions I have taken which I consider "moderate" were called "radical" by some at the time I made them. The best example of this is the proposal I made when I was a congressman during the height of the Vietnam War. I went to Canada to visit with American draft resisters who had left the United State to avoid the draft, as well as meet with deserters who had left the U.S. Armed Forces without leave and had found sanctuary in Canada. I urged that they be given amnesty by the president. My proposal shocked many people, who denounced me at the time, particularly because I included deserters in the amnesty that I proposed.

The war ended in 1975, with our retreat by helicopter from Saigon to Navy ships well covered by television. In 1977, newly elected President Jimmy Carter issued an amnesty covering most draft dodgers and deserters. So, a proposal that appeared radical at the time it was offered becomes, in hindsight, moderate, meaning it is acceptable to a majority of our people.

What am I trying to convey here? People in office are worried to death about changing their long-held positions. They know the power of the word "flip-flop." Be not afraid as long as you ground your change in logic, common sense, and change in circumstances.

An important part of being a leader in politics or business involves recognizing when conditions have changed and a new course is required. This is common sense, not "flip-flopping," and it will be acknowledged as such. It is when a leader blindly sticks with a losing policy that people begin to lose confidence. The ability to intelligently adapt to an ever-changing world and remain true to your own values and beliefs creates the best buzz, the buzz that says, "You can't go wrong following that person; he (or she) is on top of things."

Change Can Be Good

Many people do not welcome change. Depending on the circumstances, being open to change can mean the difference between success and a serious letdown in a community. Keep in mind that life is dynamic, not static.

Let me say without arrogance that I read six or more newspapers every day. That keeps me on top of events. The *New York Times* is first, the *New York Post* second, followed by the *New York Sun*, the *Daily News*, *Forward*, *Newsday*, and the *Wall Street Journal*. Reading all these papers takes me roughly three hours over the course of the day.

I share this with you because what I am doing is really preparing for my Friday-night Bloomberg Radio call-in show. With pride I say there hasn't been a call to which I did not have an intelligent, knowledgeable response. By keeping abreast of the news, I am informed and well prepared for questions from reporters or callers on my radio programs, and I am able to write educated Commentaries on subjects where I would like to see change take place.

Change is inevitable. *Comparing what happened in the past to what is happening now may help you realize what is going to happen next. I am not clairvoyant, but I do have enough hindsight to help me have foresight, and I do this by remaining informed through the newspapers I read.*

Stay educated and informed in your field of choice, whatever it may be. Knowledge is the key. After I lost the Assembly election in 1962, a good friend of mine said to me, knowing it would really hurt, "You have the attention span of a flea." She wanted to spur me on to become more knowledgeable, and her comment did just that.

In addition to reading the newspapers, I enjoy brainstorming with friends and associates. I have had a Saturday lunch meeting with six to eight friends every week for nearly thirty-five years. We meet at my home; because Gracie Mansion was my home for twelve years, we met there while I was mayor. We meet at noon, schmooze for an hour or so and then leave for lunch at some small restaurant. The bill, split among those present, averages about $30 per person. Don't shy away from the expenditure. It's well worth considering what you learn at such regular conclaves. Of course, the value increases with the common sense and intelligence of your circle of friends.

Visualizing the end result *is a helpful way to ascertain your goals being met while accepting the change that is taking place.*

Sometimes you may need to open yourself up to a new way of thinking. If you don't, you'll siphon off your ability to advance and grow. One great benefit to life is when you wake up every morning, you don't know what's going to happen that day. Life is exciting; an open mind does not sit back and wait for success to happen.

In order to be open to change, *you must be knowledgeable, flexible, creative, goal-oriented, and directed to* *move forward with the vision of what you want to create in your life.*

Sometimes change brings about difficult issues that you have to tackle. This can only be done with an open mind so that you can devise the most effective and efficient solution to possible challenges.

Here are some of my suggestions for dealing with change:

- Keep your mind wide open. It translates into getting ready for new opportunities.
- Don't be afraid to take chances.
- When dealing with change, what happens too often is a rush to judgment. Review the pros and cons of each situation in order to learn from them and make an intelligent decision while being open to change.
- Keep your courage. Stay strong, but don't let your ego rule.
- It's okay to feel uncomfortable. Many people get too comfortable in a routine and do not want to change. They

One idea for business owners is to brainstorm with employees to turn change into opportunity. When you develop a culture of brainstorming and provide yourself and your coworkers with the tools and time to generate ideas, you give yourself an edge over others in your field.

have been "successful" by always doing things the same way, and therefore they do not see why they should change. Then there are others who change too often. Change should be deliberate.

- Remember that new opportunities depend a lot on timing. Things to consider include being in the right place at the right time.
- Don't try to force change. That can mean being in the wrong place at the wrong time. Evaluate the opportunity and ask yourself, "Is that opportunity really right for me, or am I engaging in wishful thinking?"
- Understand your strengths and weaknesses as well as your potential. If your mind is not open, you will not be able to soar to the greatest heights. Losers ignore their potential.

Living with Change

I would advise those of you facing changes, along with keeping your mind open, to focus on your strengths. The way you view yourself makes all the difference in the world. And remember, what worked before might not work now. Open your mind to new opportunities and new ways of doing things.

Here are a few questions you can ask yourself as you navigate your way through change—be it from a job loss, a promotion, a change of jobs, or a new political position:

- How do I affect others?
- Do I like the work I am doing now?
- What are the qualities about the job that I like or dislike?
- Where do I get my inspiration?
- What is my definition of success?
- What challenges me?

- What have I had to overcome to get here?
- What is my potential?
- What type of people do I want on my team?
- How will I direct that team?

Real success in creating buzz *comes from developing your core strengths. Amplify your strengths by loving what you do.*

I absolutely love doing what I am doing. I'm always learning and teaching others. Recently, I was delighted when a fellow gym member came over to me in the locker room and said, "Mayor, I have to tell you. You are everywhere, on the TV, radio, front page of the *New York Times*. Your Commentaries and movie reviews are very interesting. If people half your age produced what you do, this would be an even better place. God bless you."

God has been very good to me. The people of the City of New York have been very good to me as well. When in 1989 they decided that three terms as mayor were enough, they were right. Years later some suggested jocularly that I run again. I responded, also jocularly, "No, the people threw me out, and now the people must be punished." The people have given me and continue to give me their respect and affection, more than I would have ever hoped for. I will spend my remaining days in their service. I owe them everything.

Index

About the Authors

During his three terms as mayor from 1978 through 1989, Mayor Edward I. Koch saved the City of New York from bankruptcy, restored fiscal stability to the City of New York, and was responsible for placing the City on a GAAP (Generally Accepted Accounting Practices) balanced-budget basis. He created a housing program that, over a ten-year period, provided more than 250,000 units of affordable housing, financed by city funds in the amount of $5.1 billion. He created—for the first time in New York City—a merit judicial selection system.

Prior to being mayor, Mr. Koch served for nine years as a Congressman and two years as a member of the New York City Council. He attended City College of New York from 1941 to 1943. In his last year of college, he was drafted into the Army, where he served with the 104th Infantry Division. He received two battle stars, the Combat Infantry badge, and was honorably discharged with the rank of Sergeant in 1946. In that year, he also attended the New York University School of Law. He received his LLB degree in 1948 and began to practice law immediately thereafter.

He is currently a partner in the law firm of Bryan Cave LLP. He hosts a Friday evening call-in radio program on Bloomberg AM 1130 (WBBR) and is also a commentator on that same station. Mr. Koch is a weekly guest on NY1 television with former Senator Alfonse D'Amato, writes a weekly column for the *New York Press*, and publishes movie reviews, which appear in two newspapers. He also lectures around the country. In 2004, Mr. Koch was appointed by Secretary of State Colin L. Powell as chairman of the U.S. Delegation to the Conference on Anti-Semitism, sponsored by the Organization for Security and Co-operation in Europe (OSCE). In April 2005 he was appointed to the United States Holocaust Memorial Council by President George W. Bush for a five-year term.

Additionally, Mr. Koch is the author of numerous books, which include *Mayor; Politics; His Eminence and Hizzoner; All the Best; Citizen Koch; Ed Koch on Everything; Giuliani: Nasty Man; I'm Not Done Yet: Remaining Relevant;* and most recently, *Eddie, Harold's Little Brother,* a children's book, which he co-authored with his sister, Pat Koch Thaler. He lives in New York City.

Christy Heady is an award-winning, best-selling author of three books, including *The Complete Idiot's Guide to Making Money on Wall Street* and *The Complete Idiot's Guide to Managing Your Money.* Her professional background includes fifteen years in television production and reporting experience for CNN, PAX-TV, CBS, and ABC. Her print work has been featured in publications such as *NewsMax,* the *Chicago Tribune,* the *Christian Science Monitor,* and *Consumers Digest.* Heady earned her B.A. degree in Communications from Loyola University of Chicago and a Film Studies certificate from Florida International University in Miami. She lives in North Palm Beach, Florida.